Fundamentals of Psychological
and
Educational Measurement

Fundamentals of Psychological
and
Educational Measurement

By

HERMAN R. TIEDEMAN

Professor of Psychology, Emeritus
Illinois State University
Normal, Illinois

CHARLES C THOMAS • PUBLISHER
Springfield · Illinois · U.S.A.

Published and Distributed Throughout the World by
CHARLES C THOMAS · PUBLISHER
BANNERSTONE HOUSE
301-327 East Lawrence Avenue, Springfield, Illinois, U.S.A.
NATCHEZ PLANTATION HOUSE
735 North Atlantic Boulevard, Fort Lauderdale, Florida, U.S.A.

© *1972, by* CHARLES C THOMAS · PUBLISHER
ISBN 0-398-02429-4
Library of Congress Catalog Card Number: 70-184614

With THOMAS BOOKS *careful attention is given to all details of
manufacturing and design. It is the Publisher's desire to present books
that are satisfactory as to their physical qualities and artistic possibilities
and appropriate for their particular use.* THOMAS BOOKS *will be true
to those laws of quality that assure a good name and good will.*

To
Donna and Carolyn

PREFACE

THE main purpose of this book is to supply the basic techniques for the teacher and counselor to help the individual child by discovering his strengths and weaknesses. Likewise, the strength and weaknesses of a school grade, schools or a group of schools combined can be analyzed.

This important phase of making objective observations is the foundation of an effective guidance program. It provides a basis for supplementation with observations that make it possible to work closely with the individual in a personal and private manner.

The systematic procedures for making observations may aid in curriculum revision and in establishing a change in goals or a shift in emphasis in the teaching situation.

The content of this book is based on several years work in directing evaluation programs in school systems, teaching courses in psychological and educational measurement and as director of the Illinois State University Test Service. The content is the information that students and former students desired to have available in book form.

For permission to reproduce materials, grateful acknowledgment is made to Harcourt, Brace and World, Inc., Houghton Mifflin Company and to Dr. E. D. Fitzpatrick.

Data for tables and figures were provided extensively by former students who obtained them from their classrooms. The author's point of view is greatly influenced by Dr. H. A. Greene. Many colleagues assisted me in this text, and I am especially indebted to Dr. Stanley S. Marzolf for reading much of the manuscript and for his valuable suggestions.

HERMAN R. TIEDEMAN

CONTENTS

Fundamentals of Psychological
and
Educational Measurement

1 THE GROWTH OF MEASUREMENT

ENUMERATION is the result of counting, and it dates back to the beginning of history. The concept of measurement is of slightly more recent origin. Measurement is based on comparison with a standard, and it gives us the idea of "how much," as it pertains to the significance of a raw score. A raw score is a quantitative value obtained on a test to which no modification or correction has been applied.

The first written examinations apparently were used in China before the year 2,000 B.C. These essay examinations were used in screening officials for public office.

Individual differences in general have been recognized for hundreds of years, but not in a specific manner until the Greenwich Observatory incident in 1795. One observer was released from the staff because his observation did not agree with that of his co-worker. However, it was not recognized until 1822 that the reaction time of the astronomical observers differed. The time error in observations among individuals and also in the same observer is called the "personal equation."

The first psychological laboratory was established at Leipzig by W. Wundt in 1879. One of America's great psychologists was J. McKeen Cattell who did his graduate work under Wundt. He chose as his research problem the area of individual differences.

Cattell was eager that psychology be based on experimentation and measurement. In 1890 he proposed a series of "mental" tests:[1]

    I. Dynamometer Pressure
   II. Rate of Movement
  III. Sensation-areas
  IV. Pressure Causing Pain

1. Otis, A. S.: *Mind*, 1890, vol. 15, p. 373.

    V. Least Noticeable Difference in Weight
    VI. Reaction-time for Sound
   VII. Time for Naming Colours
  VIII. Bi-section of a 50 cm. line
    IX. Judgment of 10 Seconds Time
    X. Number of Letters Remembered on Once Hearing

J. McKeen Cattell recognized that his series of proposed tests ranged from bodily reactions through psychophysical to mental measurements (simple memory). It was his work in the differences in reaction time that marked the beginning of the development of mental tests in the United States.

One should note that Cattell was associated with Galton which had a strong influence on his interest in individual differences. Galton used the questionnaire method for measuring individual differences and he used instruments for studying differences in sensation and hearing. He used, for example, the "Galton whistle" for determining the highest possible audible tone.

From 1890 until Binet started work on his scales, researchers including Bagley, Bolton, Bryan, Chrisman, Wissler, and Seashore concentrated mostly on physical tests, reaction time, and simple memory tests. Binet published his first scale of mental ability in 1905. This scale introduced the idea of mental measurements or measuring higher mental processes. It yielded a total score based on a scaled series of 30 tests. Some of the tests consisted of several subtests. The Binet-Simon Scale of 1908 embodied the mental age concept and it became a significant instrument for research. Binet's third scale, which was published in 1911, retained the MA concept, and the scale was his last contribution toward the development of psychological measurement.

CONVERTED SCORES

Wilhelm Stern is recognized as having originated the ratio IQ concept in 1912. He used the terms "intelligenzalter" and "lebensalter," which when translated are mental age and chronological age. Bobertag, however, introduced the abbreviations IA and LA which in English are MA and CA. Terman applied the index MA/CA to his individual mental test in 1916, which was called the Stanford Revision of the Binet Scales. He used the date of birth as a reference point with years and months as units of measurement.

The two common methods of changing obtained scores into mental age values were age-level scaling and point scaling. Age-level scaling requires that test items be selected that are appropriate for a given age level, but not of the same difficulty. If a specific age-level population were used, for example 10-0 to 10-11, the percentage passing the item should be larger than 50 percent. The Binet-Simon Scale of 1908 classifies each test under a specific age level.

The point scale procedure first reported by Yerkes, Bridges, and Hardwick in 1915 (*A Point Scale for Measuring Mental Ability*, Warwick and York, Baltimore) is a form of arranging the items of a test in approximately their order of difficulty. Their scale, published in 1915, consisted of 20 tests. Nineteen of them were obtained from the Binet Scales. The total credit for passing items or portions of tests is based on an accumulation of points or partial credit. These points were then converted to mental age equivalents.

Up to about 1920, Thorndike and his students used the variability of persons within a grade for the purpose of making raw scores meaningful. Terman concentrated on a year and /or subdivision of a year with the time of birth as a point of departure. Limitations of both methods were then and still are recognized. There were other units of mental measurement and reference points, but those used by Thorndike and Terman reached the high point about 1922 when McCall made an important contribution. McCall based his point of departure on Thorndike's method of equal units of measurement of a difficulty scale and on Terman's units of measurement based on the chronological age.

STANDARD SCORE AS A UNIT OF MEASUREMENT

The T-score developed by McCall[2] involved several specific procedures. He arranged the total number of test items done correctly in terms of unit intervals from 0 down to the largest score obtained. For each total number of items correct, he took the number of scores (starting at the bottom of the distribution) exceeding the given score plus one-half of those obtaining the given score. The next step involved dividing the numerical value arrived at by N, which

2. McCall, William A.: *How to Measure in Education.* New York, Macmillan, 1922, Ch. X.

value was then expressed as a percent. Below (Table I) is an example for a class of twenty students using scores such as may be obtained today.

McCall recognized the point of reference as the mean of twelve-year-olds, and he observed that a pupil who obtained a scaled score of 40 would show ability one SD or 10 units below the mean. He, however, chose the zero point as 5 SD below the mean and the 100 point as 5 SD* above the mean. Each SD value contained 10 units.

TABLE I

CALCULATIONS BASED ON McCALL'S PROCEDURES

Correct Items	N	Number of Scores Exceeding Plus ½ Reaching	Percent	Scale Score
41	1	19.5	97.5	31
42	2	18.0	90	37
43	1	16.5	82.5	41
44	2	15.0	75	43
45	3	12.5	62.5	47
46	1	10.5	52.5	49
47	2	9.0	45	51
48	3	6.5	32.5	54
49	2	4.0	20	58
50	2	2.0	10	63
51	1	.5	2.5	70
52	0			

McCall assumed a normal (bell-shaped) distribution with each T-score being one-tenth of a standard deviation. He did not favor reporting scores in positive and negative or decimal values. He multiplied his standard deviation, which he obtained from tables, by 10 to remove the decimal point, and these SD values were the equivalent of T-scores.

The percentage values in McCall's tables are arranged in inverse order from what is shown in present day tables of corresponding values of standard deviations and percentiles of the normal probability curve. Consequently, a McCall "standard deviation value" of 60 (SD 6.0 X 10) is 60 units above zero. This corresponds to 1.0 stand-

---

*SD may be defined as a measure of variability with 1 SD above the mean to 1 SD below the mean including approximately 68% of the scores.

ard deviation above 0.0 on present day tables, which date from the time of Karl Pearson. On the McCall table, a SD value of 60 represents a percentile value of 15.87. When 15.87 is subtracted from 100, the difference is 84.13 which corresponds to 1.0 sigma above the mean when the mean corresponds to 0.0 sigma. McCall then had normalized standard scores with a mean of 50 and a standard deviation of 10.

McCall's standard deviation values can be related to any table of corresponding values of standard deviations and percentiles of the normal probability curve. For example, −4.0 sigmas corresponds to a sigma of 1.0 on the McCall table; −3.0 sigmas corresponds to a sigma of 2.0; −2.0 sigmas corresponds to a sigma of 3.0; −1.0 sigmas corresponds to a sigma of 4.0; 0.0 sigmas corresponds to a sigma of 5.0; 1.0 sigmas would correspond to a sigma of 6.0 on the McCall table, and so on up to 10 sigmas or the 100 point on the McCall scale.

It should be noted that McCall's percentage values are based upon the percent of cases, from lowest to highest, that lie above each succeeding higher score. If we were to establish T-scores by using the procedures illustrated in Table I in preference to the procedure based on percentile norms described later, it would be necessary to subtract the "percent" values in column 4, Table I, from 100 and use that value to convert to T-scores from a table of corresponding values of sigmas and percentiles (see Appendix A).

The T-score was named by McCall in honor of Thorndike and Terman, and it became the basis for a large variation in the designation of standard scores on achievement and psychological tests.

PSYCHOLOGICAL TESTS FOLLOWING WORLD WAR II

The term psychological tests may include tests of mental ability, special aptitude, interest inventories, personality inventories of a comparatively simple structure to the clinical types involving self report, tests of a relatively unstructured nature and projective techniques. It is the purpose of this discussion to lay the foundations for the use of and a sound interpretation of data made available by group tests of scholastic ability.

Group tests of mental ability were not generally used before 1917. Arthur S. Otis, however, had material plans for group tests that were influenced by the content of the Stanford-Binet of 1916. He made his achievements available to a Committee on the Psychological

TABLE II

SHOWING THE LOCATION OF THE VARIOUS TESTS IN SIX
INTELLIGENCE EXAMINATIONS

Type of Test	Alpha	Haggerty Delta 2	Illinois	Natl. A	Natl. B	Otis	Terman
1 Analogies	7	—	1	—	4	7	7
2 Arithmetic computation	—	—	—	—	1	—	—
3 Arithmetic problems	2	2	2	1	—	5	5
4 Best answer	3	5	—	—	—	—	2
5 Classification	—	—	—	—	—	8	9
6 Comparison	—	—	—	—	5	—	—
7 Digit Symbol	—	—	4	5	—	—	—
8 Disarranged sentences	5	—	—	—	—	3	8
9 Verbal ingenuity	—	—	5	—	—	—	—
10 Directions	1	—	—	—	—	1	—
11 Information	8	6	3	3	2	—	4
12 Number series completion	6	—	—	—	—	—	10
13 Picture completion	—	3	—	—	—	—	—
14 Sentence completion	—	—	—	2	—	9	—
15 Sentence meaning	—	1	—	—	3	—	6
16 Synonym-antonym	4	4	7	4	—	2	3
Proverbs	—	—	—	—	—	4	—
Memory	—	—	—	—	—	10	—
Geometrical forms	—	—	—	—	—	6	—
Arithmetic ingenuity	—	—	6	—	—	—	—

Examination of Recruits[3] of which Yerkes was chairman. The Otis Scale and Arthur S. Otis had a very significant influence on the structure and content of the Army Scale and its revision, the Army Alpha Group Intelligence Test. To facilitate testing illiterates, the Army Beta (nonverbal) was developed. Immediately after the war, several tests that resembled the Army Alpha Examination were developed. These included the Haggerty Intelligence Examination, Delta

3. Monroe, W. S., DeVoss, and Kelly: *Educational Tests and Measurements*, New York, Houghton Mifflin, 1924, p. 352.

2; National Intelligence Tests, Scales A and B; Illinois General Intelligence Scale; Terman Group Test of Mental Ability; and the Otis Group Intelligence Scale, Advanced. The last named was followed in 1922 by the Otis Self-Administering Tests of Mental Ability, Intermediate and Higher Examinations. The examinations were modeled after a group test of mental ability devised by Otis in January, 1918. The manual[4] (Revised, 1928) that accompanied the Otis S-A Tests of Mental Ability contains detailed data for interpreting scores including T-scores, MA, IQ (Ratio IQ and a form of DIQ), IB, PR, and classification (ability groups).

RECENT DEVELOPMENTS

Tests in use by 1922 contained a variety of types of items. An excellent summary is presented in a table by Monroe, DeVoss, and Kelly[5] (see Table II on opposite page), which shows the extent to which test authors used various type tests.

Except for factored tests, verbal and quantitative scores, verbal and nonverbal scores, and differential aptitude tests, no great changes have taken place in the nature of the content of scholastic ability tests.

GENERAL REFERENCES

Anastasi, Anne: *Psychological Testing*, 3rd ed. New York, Macmillan, 1968, pp. 3-20.

Freeman, Frank S.: *Theory and Practice of Psychological Testing*, 3rd ed. Chicago, Holt, Rinehart and Winston, 1962, pp. 1-23.

Goodenough, Florence L.: *Mental Testing*, New York, Rinehart and Company, Inc., 1949, pp. 20-94.

Greene, Harry A. *et al.*: *Measurement and Evaluation in the Elementary School*, 2nd ed. New York, Longmans, Green and Co., 1953, pp. 19-36.

Ross, C. C. and Julian C. Stanley: *Measurement in Today's Schools*, 3rd ed. New York, Prentice-Hall, 1954, pp. 27-59.

Thorndike, Robert L. and Elizabeth Hagen: *Measurement and Evaluation in Psychology and Education*, 2nd ed. New York, John Wiley and Sons, 1961, pp. 1-16.

4. *Otis S-A Tests of Mental Ability, Manual of Directions.* World Book Company, 1922, 1928.

5. Monroe, *op. cit.*: p. 361. Reproduced by permission of Houghton Mifflin.

2 TEST NORMS

THE most commonly used converted score for interpreting test results at the elementary school level is the grade equivalent, also called grade placement. Usually the raw scores and their grade equivalents or grade placements are set up in the form of a norm or norms table. In the case of norms, an average or measure of central tendency such as the mean or median is used as the point of departure. It is common practice to interpolate the intervals between the successive averages between grades for each tenth of an interval. This is quite logical since most school systems operate on a nine months per school year basis. For example, at the beginning of the school year a pupil in grade six would have an actual grade placement of 6.0, following the first two weeks his actual grade placement would be 6.1 and it would remain that until six weeks of the term had elapsed. Then for the following four weeks his actual grade placement would be 6.2, etc. The last two weeks of the ninth month his actual grade placement would be 6.9. With the introduction of computers and electronic test scoring machines, it has become a fairly common practice to omit the decimal point between the grade and school month. A grade equivalent of 62, for example, should be interpreted to mean grade six second month.

Should local grade norms be desired for one or more tests it can be done by turning the test scores into grade equivalents. The same procedure can be applied by using the scores obtained on a standardized test or a locally constructed test. The reliability of the test and norms have an important bearing on the value of the grade equivalents. This is one of several procedures used to attach meaning to test scores.

Extrapolated values may be obtained mathematically by fitting a curve to the available data or as is more frequently done, by using a graphic representation. Extrapolated values may not be too reliable.

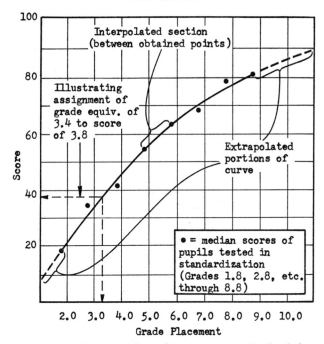

Figure 1. Sample grade norm line, for a test standardized in grades 1 through 8, illustrating extrapolation and interpolation, and process of assigning grade equivalents.

A good example of determining interpolated and extrapolated values is shown by the above graphic representation.[6]

The data in Table III illustrate how to establish grade equivalent norms from each point score on a test. The difference between the norm (median or mean) for grade five, 17, and the norm for grade six, 28, is 11 units. This range in tenths must be divided into 11 equal distances. The rate used in determining the grade equivalents between grade five (5.0) and grade six (6.0) is 1/11 which is .0909 grade units. An increase of one score value from 17 to 18 adds .0909 to grade 5.0 which results in a grade equivalent of 5.1. Adding the rate once more to correspond to a score of 19 increases the grade equivalent to 5.2 units. The same procedure is used throughout. A new rate must be established since there may be a different number of score values between grade norms (i.e. 6.0 to 7.0) as

6. Lennon, R.T.: *Test Service Notebook* 13. Test Department, Harcourt, Brace and World, Inc. Reproduced by permission of the publisher.

in our illustration. The rate in this case is 1/14 which is .07142. When adding the rate, five digits beyond the decimal point are used, but in establishing the grade equivalent only the two digits beyond the decimal point in the index value column are considered. The procedure* as outlined above may be used with points of departure such as 4.6, 5.6, 6.6.

TABLE III

ILLUSTRATION TO SHOW HOW TO ESTABLISH GRADE
EQUIVALENT NORMS

Score on Test X	Grade Equivalent	Index Value Added to Mean Score	Score on Text X	Grade Equivalent	Index Value Added to Mean Score
17	5.0		30	6.1	28.14284
18	5.1	17.0909	31	6.2	28.21426
19	5.2	17.1818	32	6.3	28.28568
20	5.3	17.2727	33	6.4	28.35710
21	5.4	17.3636	34	6.4	28.42852
22	5.5	17.4545	35	6.5	28.49994
23	5.5	17.5454	36	6.6	28.57136
24	5.6	17.6363	37	6.6	28.64278
25	5.7	17.7272	38	6.7	28.71420
26	5.8	17.8181	39	6.8	28.78562
27	5.9	17.9090	40	6.9	28.85704
28	6.0		41	6.9	28.92846
29	6.1	28.07142	42	7.0	

Rate 5.0 to 6.0 = 1/11 = .09090
Rate 6.0 to 7.0 = 1/14 = .07142

DETERMINING GRADE NORMS

Grade norms are by far the most commonly used type of norms for interpreting standardized achievement tests in the elementary grades. Norms as indicated above are available for each month of the school year. Grade equivalents are rarely used with high school tests as most high school subjects are of relatively short duration and some do not have a specific grade location.

The chief advantage of grade scores or grade equivalents is that they are easily understood. There are, however, a number of limitations. Some of the limitations are (1) grade placements are usually not comparable on different tests; (2) as demonstrated above they are based on the average score obtained by the pupils of a

*Procedure used by H. A. Greene: *Work-Book in Educational Measurements and Evaluation.* New York, Longmans, Green and Co., 1945, p. 90.

given grade time; (3) they appear to possess a mathematical precision which existing test reliabilities do not warrant; (4) on some tests the grade placement values are comparatively unreliable at both ends of the distribution of scores.

It may be said that a child who has an actual grade placement of 5.2 but obtains a grade placement score of 7.1 has obtained a grade placement score that is equal to the score obtained by the average seventh grader in his first month of the school year on a given test. It should not be said that "he is the equivalent of a seventh grader."

The leading publishers of single subject or batteries of tests have in recent years published a variety of norm values. Their manuals for administration and interpretation and the technical manuals that are made available include, along with grade norms, conveniently arranged tables that make it possible to translate raw scores into standard scores (sometimes called converted scores), grade scores, grade equivalents, stanines, and percentile ranks. Grade equivalent has reference to the score obtained by pupils at a specific actual grade placement. Grade scores do not contain decimal points but with the placement of a decimal point before the last digit they are translated into grade equivalents.

PSYCHOLOGICAL TESTS

The psychological test norms will at this phase of the discussion be confined to scholastic aptitude tests. Other terms used are intelligence tests, academic aptitude tests, tests of mental ability and tests of ability to learn. Observations made in a university test service over a period of ten years indicated that in over eighty-five percent of the occasions when conferences were had with public school personnel (including counselors and classroom teachers) the most commonly used expression was "IQ Tests." The term "tests of mental ability" was used by Arthur S. Otis in 1922 as part of the title of his Self-Administering Test.

For a number of years after Wilhelm Stern advanced the IQ concept, it was common practice for most test authors to make provisions for finding the ratio IQ (RIQ) which was obtained by dividing the mental age by the chronological age, and the quotient was multiplied by 100 to remove the decimal point. The mental age norm values were established by finding the average score obtained on the test or tests by successive chronological age groups. For example, if children with a chronological age of seven years and six months obtained an average score of 32 on a test, the mental age equivalent for a score of 32 was 7-6.

The MA indicates the level of mental maturity that the pupil has reached and the IQ is an index of relative brightness that is based on a test of mental ability and chronological age. The traditional IQ was based on the assumption that a straight line relationship existed between the MA and CA.

The observation has been made for many years that when mental growth is placed on some scale of equal units the results form a curved line with a gradual slowing down of the rate of development. Boynton[7] shows a mental growth curve based on mental age and life age suggested by Bobertag in 1911. Furthermore the shape of the curve is affected by the level of ability of the individual. The shape of the mental growth curve is well illustrated by Kuhlmann[8] for below average, average and above average persons. He constructed the growth curves on the basis of the Heinis mental growth units (called PC). Cattell[9] has shown that the Heinis PC is not as constant as the IQ for persons of high intelligence as it is for those of low intelligence.

With the rapid change in the approach to the IQ concept test, publishers and authors are changing to a standard score to arrive at a "deviation IQ," or DIQ. The T-score, which is a modification of McCall's T-score, is used as the basis for the DIQ technique. The simple formula used is

$$DIQ = \frac{(X - M)\ 16}{\sigma_{dist}} + 100$$

(where X is a score, M the mean and σ_{dist} is the SD of the distribution). The results resemble the RIQ in that the average score is 100 and the standard deviation is 16 (or it could be made more

7. Boynton, Paul L.: *Psychology of Child Development*, Minneapolis, Minnesota, Educational Publishers, Inc., 1938, p. 191.

8. Kuhlmann, F. and Rose Anderson: *Kuhlmann-Anderson Intelligence Tests—Instruction Manual.* Minneapolis, Minnesota, Educational Test Bureau, 1927, 1942, p. 18.

9. Cattell, Psyche: "The Heinis Personal Constant as a Substitute for the IQ," *Journal of Educational Psychology*, 24: 221-228, 1933.

or less than 16). The DIQ has all the advantages of standard scores and persons using the test results have a feeling of familiarity with them.

Percentile rank norm charts were made available by Otis[10] almost fifty years ago. One of the more recent type norms to be included in group test manuals is the stanine which is a form of standard score.

The mathematical techniques used to establish norms and the use and interpretation of test scores will be presented in the following chapters.

GENERAL REFERENCES

Anastasi, Anne: *Psychological Testing*, 3rd ed. New York, Macmillan, 1968, pp. 39-67.

Cronbach, Lee J.: *Essentials of Psychological Testing*, 2nd ed. New York, Harper and Brothers, 1960, pp. 87-94, 385-388.

Freeman, Frank S.: *Theory and Practice of Psychological Testing*, 3rd ed. Chicago, Holt, Rinehart and Winston, 1962, pp. 120-137.

Ross, C. C. and Julian C. Stanley: *Measurement in Today's Schools*, 3rd ed. New York, Prentice-Hall, 1954, pp. 274-300.

Standards for Educational and Psychological Tests and Manuals. Washington, D. C., American Psychological Association, Inc., 1966, pp. 33-35.

Thorndike, Robert L. and Elizabeth Hagen: *Measurement and Evaluation in Psychology and Education*, 2nd ed. New York, John Wiley and Sons, 1961, pp. 124-159.

10. Otis, Arthur: *Otis Self-Administering Tests of Mental Ability-Interpretation Charts.* World Book Company, 1922, p. 4.

3 SCORES AND THE FREQUENCY DISTRIBUTION

W HEN a test is scored, the numerical value obtained or assigned to it is a raw score. The raw score may be converted to some derived score as described in Chapter 7. Scores on objective tests may be the number right or correction for chance may be applied. Tests that are of the performance type have the results quantified in terms of errors or time. Essay tests may be grouped in terms of quality and some form of quantitative value assigned to each group.

When students are told not to guess, the reliability of the test is slightly higher. Observations by Greene,[11] made largely from a study by Ruch and Stoddard, indicate that if all students had answered all items on a test and the test scored for rights only and then scored again with correction for guessing, the relative positions of the students in the two distributions of scores would not have changed. The "correction for guessing formula" that is used is

$$\text{Score} = R - \frac{W}{N-1}$$

(R, number right; W, number wrong; N, number of foils per item). On the IBM Optical Mark Reader there are controls so that the machine can be instantly adjusted for $R - W$, $R - 1/3W$, $R - 1/4W$, R only, W only, or Omits only. The implication when using a correction formula is that all foils at the end of an item are equally plausible. This usually is not the case as the examinee may, without much hesitation, eliminate one or more foils as not being an answer to the item.

CONCEPT OF SCORES IN A FREQUENCY DISTRIBUTION

It is necessary to point out more specifically a characteristic of scores in psychological data. A score of 17 (whole number), when

11. Greene, Edward B.: *Measurements of Human Behavior*, Rev. ed. New York, Odysses Press, 1952, pp. 70-76.

unit intervals in a frequency distribution are used, includes the numerical values from 16.50 *to* 17.50 or 16.50-17.49. The fractional limits usually are not shown but must be recognized in mathematical operations. The data in test score distributions usually are continuous rather than discrete data. We might say that fractional limits are "real" limits and that our score of 17 is the midpoint of a scale unit. Likewise if we had a class interval of 69-71 the lower limit would be considered 68.5 for mathematical calculations and the midpoint of the interval would be 70. With the size of the interval being 3, five-tenths of 3 is 1.5, and 1.5 added to the lower limit of interval 69-71 is 68.5 + 1.5 or 70 which is the midpoint of the interval.

THE FREQUENCY DISTRIBUTION

A mass of scores is relatively meaningless. To make them meaningful, it becomes necessary to organize the data by placing them into a frequency distribution. The frequency table or distribution shows roughly the characteristics of the distribution, but more important, it makes the data or scores more amenable to further statistical treatment.

The scores in Table IV are those obtained by two classes on a history test. These same scores will be used to illustrate the use of several different types of calculations to help in the use and interpretation of test scores.

TABLE IV

SCORES OBTAINED ON A U. S. HISTORY TEST

99	78	72	75	69	66	60	97	98	95	95	90
86	89	89	88	91	88	91	86	86	86	74	81
96	93	90	84	92	87	83	78	94	68	69	79
81	82	87	81	84	83	76	75	80	79	70	80
82	82	85	85	78	83	77	76	77	72	71	73
67											

To set up a frequency distribution* certain steps can easily be followed to facilitate organization and make for efficiency. The steps are as follows:

1. *Find the range*—this is found by subtracting the smallest score from the largest score. In certain mathematical applications, the total range may

*Grouping of data may be unnecessary where computer or programmable calculators are available.

be desired which consists of adding 1 to the range. The total range is not necessary when setting up a frequency distribution in psychological measurement.

2. *Size and number of steps in the distribution*—divide the range by 15 and select the nearest whole odd number as the size of the class interval. This usually yields between 12 to 18 class intervals. Fewer than 12 intervals may introduce a significant grouping error. If the obtained quotient is an even number, e.g. 4, we would try 5 as the size of our interval and if that would not yield at least 12 steps we would use 3 as the size of our interval even though it resulted in more than 18 steps or intervals. This frequently occurs when unit intervals are involved.

3. *Limits of intervals*—the lower limit of the top interval is an odd number just large enough so that the largest score obtained could be tabulated in that interval. Let us assume that the largest score obtained on a test is 71 and the size of the interval is a multiple of 3; the lower limit of the top class interval would be 69 and the upper limit of the same interval would be 71 (69-71). The limits of the second interval from the top would be 66-88, and so on down 63-65, 60-62, 57-59, 54-56, etc. until the lowest score would be included in an interval.

To make a frequency distribution for the data in Table IV, following the procedure above, one would proceed as follows: The largest score obtained is 99 and the smallest score obtained is 60. The range would be 39 (99-60). The size of the interval is determined by dividing 39 by 15 which is 2+. Two plus is closer to 3 than it is to 1 so we choose 3 as the size of our interval. The lower limits of our intervals in this case should be a multiple of 3. The lower limit of our top class interval is 99, which by coincidence is also our largest score. The upper limit of the top class interval is 101 and the limits of the second interval from the top of the C. I. column (class interval column) has as its limits 96-98. There is no mathematical advantage in using the lower limit as a multiple of an odd number but as will be noted later it is mostly a matter of convenience. For example, the assumed mean will always be a whole number and there are no decimal score values when making a frequency polygon.

The data in Table V show the completed frequency distribution based on the procedures outlined above. The "f" in column 3 represents the number of scores in each interval and the "N" indicates the total number of cases or scores in the distribution.

TABLE V

FREQUENCY DISTRIBUTION OF SCORES IN TABLE IV

1 *Class* *Interval*	*2* *Tabulations*	*3* *f*
99-101	/	1
96- 98	/ / /	3
93- 95	/ / / /	4
90- 92	-/-/-/-/-	5
87- 89	-/-/-/-/- /	6
84- 86	-/-/-/-/- / / /	8
81- 83	-/-/-/-/- / / / /	9
78- 80	-/-/-/-/- / /	7
75- 77	-/-/-/-/- /	6
72- 74	/ / / /	4
69- 71	/ / / /	4
66- 68	/ / /	3
63- 65		0
60- 62	/	1
		$N = 61$

GROUPING ERROR

If we placed the scores 23, 22, 21, 20, 19, 18, 17, 16, 16, 15, 15, 15, 14, 14, 13, 12, 11, 10, 9, 8, and 7 into a frequency distribution consisting of unit intervals, the frequency distribution table would be represented as follows:

Class *Interval*	*Tabulations*	*f*
23	/	1
22	/	1
21	/	1
20	/	1
19	/	1
18	/	1
17	/	1
16	/ /	2
15	/ / /	3
14	/ /	2
13	/	1
12	/	1
11	/	1
10	/	1
9	/	1
8	/	1
7	/	1
		$N = 21$

In the above illustration we know the size of each score. There is no grouping error.

If we use a class interval (ci) of 3, the length of the frequency table would be shortened. The original scores are represented by the following illustration:

Class Interval	Tabulations	f
21-23	/ / /	3
18-20	/ / /	3
15-17	-/-/-/-/- /	6
12-14	/ / / /	4
9-11	/ / /	3
6- 8	/ /	2
		N = 21

Our best estimate of the size of the scores in the interval 21-23 is 22, which is the midpoint of the interval. The identity of the individual scores is lost. The best estimate of the size of the scores in the interval 15-17 is 16, which is the midpoint of that interval. If we calculated the means for the two illustrations they would be 14.33 and 15.00 respectively. The difference between the two means may be attributed to the grouping error introduced when we placed our scores in the table with the *ci* of 3. The 14.33 may be called the "true mean" and the mean 15.00 may be called the "obtained mean." There is no grouping error involved with the true mean.

GENERAL REFERENCES

Blommers, Paul and E. F. Lindquist: *Elementary Statistical Methods in Psychology and Education.* Boston, Houghton Mifflin, 1960, pp. 12-22.

Cronbach, Lee J.: *Essentials of Psychological Testing,* 2nd ed. New York, Harper and Brothers, 1960, pp. 77-79.

Ebel, Robert L.: *Measuring Educational Achievement,* Englewood Cliffs, N. J., Prentice-Hall, 1965, pp. 240-242.

Garrett, Henry E.: *Statistics in Psychology and Education,* 4th ed. New York, Longmans, Green and Co., 1953, pp. 1-9.

Greene, Harry A. *et al.: Measurement and Evaluation in the Elementary School,* 2nd ed. New York, Longmans, Green and Co., 1953, pp. 308-317.

Greene, Harry A. *et al.: Measurement and Evaluation in the Secondary School,* 2nd ed. New York, Longmans, Green and Co., 1954, pp. 312-328.

Helmstadter, G. C.: *Principles of Psychological Measurement.* New York, Appleton-Century-Crofts, 1964, pp. 41-43.

Johnson, Palmer O. and Robert W. B. Jackson: *Introduction to Statistical*

Methods. New York, Prentice-Hall, 1953, pp. 35-43.

Remmers, H. H. and N. L. Gage: *Educational Measurement and Evaluation,* Rev. ed. New York, Harper and Brothers, 1955, pp. 570-575.

Thorndike, Robert L. and Elizabeth Hagen: *Measurement and Evaluation in Psychology and Education,* 2nd ed. New York, John Wiley and Sons, 1961, pp. 96-102.

Van Dalen, Deobold B.: *Understanding Educational Research,* Enlarged and rev. ed. New York, McGraw-Hill, 1962, pp. 330-334.

4 PERCENTILES AND PERCENTILE NORMS

A percentile may be defined as a point on a scale above which and below which a certain percent of the scores in a distribution lie. The mechanical aspects involved in calculating percentile points are important, but where and how to make practical applications is even more important. Basically, performance on a test is indicated by the location of the score in a given distribution of scores. Performance on a test is made more meaningful when distributions are divided into distances so that each distance or division contains the same percentage of the total number of scores in the distribution. Examples of such divisions of distributions are quartiles, quintiles, and deciles. The distributions may also be divided into hundredths by establishing every percentile point from one through 99.

Percentile points and percentile ranks must not be confused. A percentile rank is a distance, interval, or area between two percentile points while a percentile is a point on a scale. It is not correct to say that a score lies in a quartile or a decile as both are points on a scale. It is appropriate to say that a score lies in the first quarter or that the obtained score has a decile rank of one. If the score lies in the first quarter it is below Q_1 or if the score has a decile rank of one it is below decile point one (see Table VII).

QUARTILE POINTS

The quartile points may be designated as Q_3, Mdn. (Q_2), and Q_1 or P_{75}, P_{50}, and P_{25}. The former series is preferred in psychological measurement. In a few instances, the median has been designated as Q_2. It should be recognized that the median is also an average or measure of central tendency. A percentile point could be any one of 99 percentile points.

Computing Percentile Points*

For the purpose of illustrating the computation of a percentile, the frequency distribution in Table V will be used. These scores are the same scores shown previously in Table IV. To compute, for example, Q_1 or the 25th percentile, the following steps will be used.

1. *Partial Sum* (PS). Multiply the number of cases (N) by .25 which is $61 \times .25 = 15.25$.

2. *Subtotal* (ST). The subtotal may equal but it must not exceed the PS. In our example, the ST is 12 as that is as far as we can go up in the cumulative frequency (cf) column without exceeding the value 15.25. The 25th percentile lies somewhere in the interval 75-77.

3. *Correction in terms of score* (d). This correction is 15.25 (PS) minus 12 (ST) equals 3.25 (d). This step indicates how many more scores must be added to our ST to obtain the PS.

4. *Correction in terms of interval.* This represents the proportion of the scores in the interval 75-77 that are added to the lower limit of this interval. There are 6 scores (f) in the interval 75-77, hence 3.25 is divided by 6 (d/f).

5. *Correction in terms of scale distance or size of interval.* This is

TABLE VI
COMPUTING PERCENTILE VALUES

1 Class Interval	2 f	3 cf
99-101	1	61
96- 98	3	60
93- 95	4	57
90- 92	5	53
87- 89	6	48
84- 86	8	42
81- 83	9	34
78- 80	7	25
75- 77	6	18
72- 74	4	12
69- 71	4	8
66- 68	3	4
63- 65	0	1
60- 62	1	1
	N = 61	

*Procedure based on Greene, *et al.*: *Measurement and Evaluation in the Elementary School*, 2nd ed. New York, Longmans, Green and Co., 1953, p. 325.

achieved by multiplying the correction in terms of the interval (i). The complete correction is written as $d/f \times i$. The $d \times i$ values should be obtained before the division is performed.

6. *The percentile point.* Add the correction computed to the lower limit of the interval in which the percentile lies.

Lower Quartile (Q_1)

$$PS = 15.25$$
$$ST = 12$$
$$d = \overline{3.25}$$

$$\text{Correction} = \frac{d}{f} \times i$$

$$\text{Correction} = \frac{3.25}{6} \times 3$$

$$\text{Correction} = \frac{9.75}{6} = 1.625 \text{ or } 1.63$$

$$Q_1 = 74.50 + 1.63 = 76.13$$

Median (P_{50} or Mdn)

$$PS = 30.50 \ (61 \times .50)$$
$$ST = 25.00 \ (\text{cf below interval in which Mdn lies})$$
$$d = \overline{5.50} \ (\text{correction in terms of scores})$$

$$\frac{5.50}{9} (\text{correction in terms of interval})$$

$$\frac{5.50}{9} \times 3 = \frac{16.50}{9} = 1.833 \text{ or } 1.83 \ (\text{correction in terms of scale distance})$$

$$80.50 + 1.83 = 82.33 \text{ (Median)}$$

Upper Quartile (P_{75} or Q_3)

$$PS = 45.75 \ (61 \times .75)$$
$$ST = 42 \ (\text{cf below interval in which } Q_3 \text{ lies})$$
$$d = \overline{3.75} \ (\text{correction in terms of scores})$$

$$\frac{3.75}{6} (\text{correction in terms of interval})$$

$$\frac{3.75}{6} \times 3 = \frac{11.25}{6} = 1.875 \text{ or } 1.88 \ (\text{correction in terms of scale distance})$$

$$86.50 + 1.88 = 88.38 \ (Q_3)$$

When computing percentiles it is assumed that the scores or frequencies (f) are uniformly distributed throughout each interval. The correction must be added to the *fractional* lower limit of the interval. The reason for this is described in a preceding chapter.

It is possible to work from the top of the frequency column downward. The correction is then subtracted from the upper limit of the interval in which the given percentile lies.

There are instances where the PS and ST are equal. In such cases one would assign the value of the lower fractional limit of the interval just above the PS as the numerical value of the percentile point calculated. Should the interval just above the PS contain zero frequencies when the PS and ST are equal, then one would assign the midpoint of the interval above the ST as the numerical value of the percentile point.

Quarters and Quartile Points

The quartile points may be designated as Q_3, Mdn, and Q_1. All scores from Q_3 and up lie in the fourth quarter, the scores that lie in the area from the median to Q_3 are in the third quarter, those that lie in the area from Q_1 to the median are in the second quarter, and those scores beneath Q_1 lie in the first quarter.

DECILE POINTS AND DECILE RANKS

There are nine decile points in a distribution which divide the distribution into ten equal areas. Reference to Table VII indicates that decile point 9 corresponds to percentile point 90, decile point 8 corresponds to percentile point 80, and so on. Decile rank 10 covers the percentile rank interval or area from the percentile point 90 to the percentile point 99 inclusive, decile rank 9 covers the percentile rank interval from the percentile rank point 80-89, etc.

TABLE VII

A CROSS REFERENCE PERCENTILE CHART

Decile Point	Percentile Point	Decile Rank	Percentile Rank
9	90	10	90-99
8	80	9	80-89
7	70	8	70-79
6	60	7	60-69
5	50	6	50-59
4	40	5	40-49
3	30	4	30-39
2	20	3	20-29
1	10	2	10-19
		1	1- 9

It should be noted that the decile rank one covers the percentile rank interval from 1 to 9 inclusive.

Establishing Decile Rank Norms

The steps involved in establishing decile rank norms include the same steps illustrated in computing quartiles. We would establish (see Table VII) 9 decile points by calculating percentile points 90, 80, 70, 60, 50, 40, 30, 20, and 10. For the data in Table VI, these percentile score values correspond to the same scale points. The PS for 90 is 54.90, the ST is 53, and the d is 1.90. Substituting in the formula

$$\frac{d}{f} \times i, \frac{1.90}{4} \times 3 = \frac{5.70}{4} = 1.43$$

which is the correction to be added to 92.5 which equals 93.93, and it is the score value for decile point 9 and percentile point 90. Each of the nine decile points must be likewise established. The decile points for the data in Table VIII with their respective percentile score values are (9) 93.93, (8) 89.98, (7) 86.85, (6) 84.48, (5) 82.33, (4) 80.24, (3) 77.63, (2) 74.60, (1) 70.08.

A convenient format to establish decile norms is shown in Table VIII.

TABLE VIII

FRACTIONAL AND ROUNDED LIMITS FOR ESTABLISHING DECILE RANKS

Decile Rank	Fractional Limits	Rounded Limits
10	93.93-	94-
9	89.98-93.93	90-93
8	86.85-89.98	87-89
7	84.48-86.85	85-86
6	82.33-84.48	83-84
5	80.24-82.33	81-82
4	77.63-80.24	78-80
3	74.60-77.63	75-77
2	70-08-74.60	71-74
1	-70.08	-70

The rounded limits can be observed quite readily. Decile rank 4 may serve as an illustration. The lowest score one could obtain and still have a decile rank of 4 is 78 and the highest score one could obtain and still have a decile rank of 4 is 80. (If the fractional limits for decile rank 4 had been 77.63 to 80.00, then the rounded limits for decile rank 4 would have been 78-79.)

The norm table prepared for the scores in Table IV and represented in Table VIII is set up as a simple table such as one would find in the manual for a standardized test when decile rank norms are used. The completed norm table is shown by the data in Table IX.

TABLE IX

DECILE RANK NORM TABLE BASED ON SCORES SHOWN IN TABLE IV

Scores	Decile Rank
94-	10
90-93	9
87-89	8
85-86	7
83-84	6
81-82	5
78-80	4
75-77	3
71-74	2
-70	1

PERCENTILE RANKS AND SCORES

Percentile ranks of scores or a percentile norm table can be conveniently constructed by using a frequency distribution. The data in the first three columns in Table X are identical to the data in the three columns shown in Table VI. To calculate percentile ranks of scores in grouped data, two additional columns are required. The numerical values in column 4 are based on the cumulative frequencies in column 3. As may be observed one may start at either the upper or lower end of column 4. In this illustration we will start at the bottom of the column and work upward. We are then concerned with interval 60-62. The cumulative frequency (cf) below this interval (i) is of course zero, plus one-half (.5f). The frequencies (f) in the interval would be $1 \times .5$ or 0.5 as indicated. To illustrate further consider class interval 81-83. The cf below the interval is 25, plus $.5 \times 9$ (f in the interval) or $25 + 4.5 = 29.5$, etc.

The percentile ranks in column 5 are obtained by dividing the numerical value in column 4 for each interval by N and multiplying the quotient by 100. For the interval 99-101 the numerical value $60.5 \div 61 \times 100 = 99.1$ which is then rounded to 99.

TABLE X

CALCULATION OF PERCENTILE RANKS OF SCORES IN TABLE VI

1 Class Interval	2 f	3 cf	4 cf below i + .5f	5 *Percentile Rank	
99-101	1	61	60.5	(99.1)	99
96- 98	3	60	58.5	(95.9)	96
93- 95	4	57	55.0	(90.1)	90
90- 92	5	53	50.5	(82.7)	83
87- 89	6	48	45.0	(73.7)	74
84- 86	8	42	38.0	(62.2)	62
81- 83	9	34	29.5	(48.3)	48
78- 80	7	25	21.5	(35.2)	35
75- 77	6	18	15.0	(24.5)	25
72- 74	4	12	10.0	(16.3)	16
69- 71	4	8	6.0	(9.8)	10
66- 68	3	4	2.5	(4.0)	4
63- 65	0	1	1.0	(1.6)	2
60- 62	1	1	0.5	(0.8)	1
N = 61					

$$*\frac{\text{cf below i} + .5f}{N} \times 100$$

A percentile rank or percentile norm table may be recorded in simple form as shown in Table XI which is similar to the format used in Table IX.

TABLE XI

PERCENTILE RANK OF SCORES OBTAINED ON A HISTORY
TEST AS LISTED IN TABLE IV

Scores	Percentile Rank
99-101	99
96- 98	96
93- 95	90
90- 92	83
87- 89	74
84- 86	62
81- 83	48
78- 80	35
75- 77	25
72- 74	16
69- 71	10
66- 68	4
63- 65	2
60- 62	1

Establishing Percentile Ranks for Ranked Scores

There are situations when it is convenient to calculate the percentile ranks for a group of test scores or for ratings assigned to a group of persons. The scores are ranked from 1 to nth score. The following scores provide a practical illustration in which there may be two or more identical relative ranks. Let us assume that we have scores of

53,	52,	50,	50,	49,	48,	47,	46,	45,	45,	45,	44,	43,	42,	41,	and	40
1	2	3.5	3.5	5	6	7	8	10	10	10	12	13	14	15		16

The corresponding relative ranks are indicated directly beneath the scores. (We have a total of 16 scores. We should not rank the two tied scores of 50 three and four respectively, but we add ranks 3 and 4 and divide the sum by 2

$$\frac{3+4}{2} = 3.5$$

hence the two tied scores have a rank of 3.5.) A simple formula for converting relative ranks to percentile ranks is

$$PR = 100 - \frac{(100R - 50)}{N}$$

The PR of a score of 53 is

$$100 - \frac{(100 \times 1 - 50)}{16} = 96.87 \text{ or } 97$$

For the score of 50 the PR is

$$100 - \frac{(100 \times 3.5 - 50)}{16} = 81.25 \text{ or } 81$$

For the score of 40 the PR is

$$100 - \frac{(100 \times 16 - 50)}{16} = 3.13 \text{ or } 3$$

Advantages and Limitations of Percentile Points

Percentile ranks can be quite meaningful when one interprets score values on a test to other persons. The interpretation should be based on the concept of 99 points and 100 "distances" or areas marked off by the 99 points. The percentile rank (PR) of a score indicates what percent of the scores of a given population lie below or above the given score. Direct comparisons can be made between the percentile ranks of scores obtained by a person on subtests of a test battery.

Most norm tables are based on an approximately normal distribution of scores. Hence, the absolute score values, when expressed in terms of percentile ranks, are not equally spaced from the median to either tail of the distribution. The percentile ranks would be equal only if we had a rectangular distribution of scores such as one obtains when nine decile points are established. The data in the distribution chart in Appendix A show this quite clearly. Since there are the inequalities in the distances between percentile ranks, it is generally considered not good practice to average percentile ranks.

GENERAL REFERENCES

Anastasi, Anne: *Psychological Testing*, 3rd ed. New York, Macmillan, 1968, pp. 49-52.

Blommers, Paul and E. F. Lindquist: *Elementary Statistical Methods in Psychology and Education*. Boston, Houghton Mifflin, 1960, pp. 65-79.

Cronbach, Lee J.: *Essentials of Psychological Testing*, 2nd ed. New York, Harper and Brothers, 1960, pp. 87-94.

Ebel, Robert L.: *Measuring Educational Achievement*. Englewood Cliffs, N. J., Prentice-Hall, 1965, pp. 251-263.

Ferguson, Leonard W.: *Personality Measurement*. New York, McGraw-Hill, 1952, pp. 256-262.

Freeman, Frank S.: *Theory and Practice of Psychological Testing*, 3rd ed. Chicago, Holt, Rinehart and Winston, 1962, pp. 124-127.

Garrett, Harry E., *Statistics in Psychology and Education*, 4th ed. New York, Longmans, Green and Co., 1953, pp. 66-69.

Greene, Harry A. *et al.*: *Measurement and Evaluation in the Elementary School*, 2nd ed. New York, Longmans, Green and Co., 1953, pp. 347-349.

Johnson, Palmer O. and Robert W. B. Jackson: *Introduction to Statistical Methods*. New York, Prentice-Hall, 1953, pp. 43-49.

Ross, C. C. and Julian C. Stanley: *Measurement in Today's Schools*, 3rd ed. New York, Prentice-Hall, 1954, pp. 274-279.

Thorndike, Robert L. and Elizabeth Hagen: *Measurement and Evaluation in Psychology and Education*, 2nd ed. New York, John Wiley and Sons, 1961, pp. 133-137, 153-157.

5 MEASURES OF CENTRAL TENDENCY

In a previous chapter we observed that the median is an average or measure of central tendency. The same thing can be said for the mean; it, too, is a measure of central tendency or an average. Another measure of central tendency seldom used is the mode. The midscore or counted median is sometimes used to find the "average" of subtests in a test battery.

MODE

The mode is that score in a unit interval frequency distribution that occurs the largest number of times. In ungrouped data, it is the score that occurs most frequently. When a class interval is larger than one, it is called the crude mode, and it is the midpoint of the interval that contains the largest number of scores. It is possible for a frequency distribution to have more than one mode. An estimated true mode may be obtained by the formula (3 × median) — (2 × mean). As a measure of central tendency in interpreting test scores, the mode is relatively unstable. In unit intervals, a score that occurs the largest number of times may not be anywhere near the mean or median. It is of little value when interpreting test scores.

MEAN

One method of calculating the arithmetic mean (usually called the mean) is to sum the score values and divide the sum by the number of scores or cases in the group. This is the ungrouped data method which is also called the "long method." The formula is

$$\frac{\Sigma X}{N}$$

For the data in Table IV, the sum of the 61 scores is 5008. Dividing this sum by 61 (5008 ÷ 61 = 82.0985) gives us the true mean.

The formula for the "short method" of finding the mean is

$$M = AM + \frac{\Sigma fd}{N} i$$

This formula is used when the data are grouped or placed into a frequency distribution.

The AM is the abbreviation for assumed mean. The mean may be assumed to lie at the midpoint of any interval in the frequency distribution, but it is better to assume it to lie somewhere near where one would expect the mean to lie as it reduces the size of some of the quantitative values with which one must work. This becomes obvious when observing a frequency distribution set up to calculate the mean. The correction part

$$\left(\frac{\Sigma fd}{N} i \right)$$

of the formula will correct for the amount that one has erred from the obtained mean. It makes no mathematical difference in the final answer where one assumes the mean to lie, but we must assume it to lie at the midpoint of an interval.

The class intervals and frequency columns in Table X are reproduced in Table XII.

Steps in Calculating the Mean—Grouped Data

1. Set up the frequency distribution.
2. Tabulate the scores.
3. Record the frequencies (number of scores in each interval).
4. Indicate the assumed mean (in the illustration it is 82 which is the *midpoint* of the interval 81-83).
5. Fill in the deviations from the assumed mean. Start with zero deviation which is the midpoint of the interval 81-83 which is the same point at which the assumed mean lies—hence the zero deviation. Count both up and down from the zero point to each succeeding midpoint of each interval. Above the assumed mean the deviation values are positive and below it they are negative.
6. Consider the fd column where the products of the frequencies and deviations are shown. Find the algebraic sum of the values in the fd column (positive 72 and negative 69 = 3). It is obvious that the sum of fd (Σfd) could be negative, hence it is important to observe the positive or negative sign.

TABLE XII

CALCULATION OF THE MEAN FOR DATA SHOWN IN TABLE IV

ci	Tabulations	f	d	fd
99-101	/	1	6	6
96- 98	/ / /	3	5	15
93- 95	/ / / /	4	4	16
90- 92	-/-/-/-	5	3	15
87- 89	-/-/-/- /	6	2	12
84- 86	-/-/-/- / / /	8	1	8
81- 83	-/-/-/- / / / / 9		0	(+72)
78- 80	-/-/-/- / /	7	—1	—7
75- 77	-/-/-/- /	6	—2	—12
72- 74	/ / / /	4	—3	—12
69- 71	/ / / /	4	—4	—16
66- 68	/ / /	3	—5	—15
63- 65		0	—6	0
60- 62	/	1	—7	—7
				(—69)
		N = 61		$\Sigma = +3$

$$M = AM + \frac{\Sigma fd}{N} i \quad (\Sigma fd/N = c)$$

$$M = 82 + \frac{3}{61} \times 3$$

$$M = 82 + \frac{9}{61}$$

$$M = 82 + .1475$$

$$M = 82.1475$$

7. Mean of the deviations of scores. The mean of the deviations is found by dividing Σfd by N, keeping in mind the proper sign. This facilitates locating the point on the scale where the sums of the values above and below it are equal.

8. Mean of the deviations of scores converted to scale distance. This is done by multiplying the mean of the deviations of scores (c in terms of class interval) by the size of the class interval (c in terms of scale distance). In the illustration (Table XII) the Σfd is multiplied by i (size of class interval) before dividing by N which may reduce rounding errors.

9. The arithmetic mean. The arithmetic mean is the result of combining algebraically the assumed mean and the correction. In the illustration the correction is positive so the correction of .1475 is added to the

assumed mean of 82 which gives us an obtained mean of 82.1475. (The number of places to carry digits beyond the decimal point depends upon how the results are to be used. In most of the work in psychological and educational measurement, three digits and rounded on the second is adequate.) When the "long method" ($\Sigma X/N$) or unit intervals in a frequency distribution are used, there is no grouping error and we arrive at the true mean. The use of a frequency distribution with steps larger than one unit will in all probability introduce a slight grouping error. Consequently we call the mean the "obtained" mean.

MEDIAN

The calculation of the median is shown in Chapter 4. It is one of 99 percentile points and it is the fiftieth percentile designated as mdn, P_{50}, fifth decile point, or Q_2. The symbol Q_2 is seldom used. As previously defined, the median is the percentile point on a scale above and below which fifty percent of the scores lie.

Uses of Mean and Median

The mean is affected by the scores at both the upper and lower ends of a frequency distribution while the median is unaffected. For example, if we removed the score of 60 from the interval 60-62 in Table XII and placed it in the interval 78-80 it would increase the f from 7 to 8. Recalculating the mean with this shift in scores would increase the size of the mean from 82.15 to 82.44. This points out the sensitivity of the mean to the location of the scores in a distribution.

In Chapter 4, we found the median for the same data used in Table XII to be 82.33. If, in Table XII, we kept only the interval 81-83 with a frequency of 9 and considered all the 27 frequencies above this interval to be in *any one* of the intervals above the interval 81-83 and all the 25 frequencies below the interval 81-83, our median when calculated would not change in size; it would still be 82.33. The median is not affected by the size of the scores above and below the interval in which we know the median lies.

Data that form a normal or bell-shaped distribution have identically the same mean, median, and mode. However, if a distribution is skewed (tapered) toward the higher scores, the mean will be larger than the median; and if the distribution is skewed toward the lower scores, the mean will be smaller than the median. Where more exacting measurements are involved, such as those used in research activities, the mean is preferred. The median is perhaps the best average when the classroom teacher wishes to obtain a good estimate of how her pupils are achieving as a group. When two or more classroom groups are involved in the population, the difference in choice between mean and median tends to disappear as the data usually approach a normal curve.

The basic assumptions regarding the distribution of scores within the class interval are not the same when calculating the mean and median. When calculating the mean, the assumption is that all scores in the interval lie at the midpoint of the interval. The assumption when calculating the median, or any other percentile, is that the scores are uniformly distributed throughout the interval. Hence, the term interpolation instead of correction is frequently used when calculating percentiles.

Midscore or Counted Median

The midscore or counted median is the midmost score of several subtest scores, or it could be the midmost score obtained on a test when the scores are arranged in descending or ascending order. If there were eight subtests in a test battery with scores of 28, 25, 24, 23, 22, 20, 19, and 17, the midmost score would be 22.5. When it contains a decimal value, the test manual should be consulted regarding the disposition of decimal values. It is a common practice when rounding decimal values to whole numbers in measurements to consider .5 or more a whole number. The value 22.5 if rounded would be 23.

The definition of a score that we have used in our mathematical calculations involving frequency distributions is that the score is the midpoint of a scale unit. In a previous chapter a reason given for accepting the definition was that fractional limits are "real limits." In measurements we deal mostly with continuous data and we assume that an obtained score is the best quantitative estimate of achievement.

Under certain conditions, when distributions and calculations are obtained by means of computers, fractional values are dropped. In those comparatively few instances a more appropriate definition of a score would be that the score is the lower limit of a scale unit.

The corrections in the mathematical calculations such as were applied in our frequency distributions would be made accordingly.

GENERAL REFERENCES

Blommers, Paul and E. F. Lindquist: *Elementary Statistical Methods in Psychology and Education.* Boston, Houghton Mifflin, 1960, pp. 98-133.

Ferguson, Leonard W.: *Personality Measurement.* New York, McGraw-Hill, 1952, pp. 45-58.

Freeman, Frank S.: *Theory and Practice of Psychological Testing,* 3rd ed. Chicago, Holt, Rinehart and Winston, 1962, pp. 24-30.

Goodenough, Florence L.: *Mental Testing.* New York, Rinehart and Company, 1949, pp. 175-188.

Greene, Harry A. *et al.*: *Measurement and Evaluation in the Elementary School,* 2nd ed. New York, Longmans, Green and Co., 1953, pp. 317-328.

Johnson, Palmer O. and Robert W. B. Jackson: *Introduction to Statistical Methods.* New York, Prentice-Hall, 1953, pp. 120-142.

Remmers, H. H. and N. L. Gage: *Educational Measurements and Evaluation,* Rev. ed. New York, Harper and Brothers, 1955, pp. 578-582.

Thorndike, Robert L. and Elizabeth Hagen: *Measurement and Evaluation in Psychology and Education,* 2nd ed. New York, John Wiley and Sons, 1961, pp. 103-109.

Van Dalen, Deobold B.: *Understanding Educational Research,* Enlarged and rev. ed. New York, McGraw-Hill, 1962, pp. 334-340.

6 MEASURES OF VARIABILITY

THE dispersion of the scores that make up a frequency distribution should be observed when a measure of central tendency is obtained. Measures of variability are necessary to make possible a more comprehensive observation regarding scores than could possibly be made by means of only a measure of central tendency. Two different classes may have the same means on a certain test, but one class may have both higher and lower scores than any obtained by the students in the other class.

The most frequently used measure of variability is the standard deviation. Standard deviation is basic in the establishment of derived scores that are expressed in units of the standard deviation of the scores in a given distribution. The distributions could represent the students of one class or the norming population for a standardized test. Standard deviation is also abbreviated as sigma (σ) or SD. One sigma below (-1σ) the mean to one sigma above ($+1\sigma$) the mean includes approximately the middle 68 percent of the scores. Other measures of variability are probable error, quartile deviation, average deviation, variance, and range.

COMPUTATION OF THE STANDARD DEVIATION— UNGROUPED DATA

When the definition method for finding SD is used, the formula is $\sigma = \Sigma D^2 / N$. The deviation of each score from the mean is squared (D^2), the sum of the squared value (ΣD^2) is divided by the number of scores (N) in the population ($\Sigma D^2 / N$), and the square root of the quotient is calculated

$$\sqrt{\Sigma D^2 / N}$$

The above formula is used when data are not grouped, and the procedure is sometimes called the "long method" or "definition method" of calculating SD. Standard deviation may be defined as the square root of the mean of the squares of all the deviations of the scores of a given population from the mean of the scores.

The data in Table XIII show how one would proceed to calculate sigma from ungrouped data.

TABLE XIII

CALCULATION OF THE STANDARD DEVIATION FROM UNGROUPED DATA

Score	D	D^2
38	13.27	176.09
23	—1.73	2.99
36	11.27	127.01
11	—13.73	188.51
19	—5.73	32.83
27	2.27	5.15
13	—11.73	137.59
34	9.27	85.93
15	—9.73	94.67
36	11.27	127.01
20	—4.73	22.37

$M = 24.73$ $\qquad\qquad\qquad\qquad\qquad\qquad \Sigma D^2 = 1000.15$

Substituting the appropriate values in the formula sigma $= \sqrt{\dfrac{\Sigma D^2}{N}}$

we have sigma $= \sqrt{\dfrac{1000.15}{11}}$

sigma $= \sqrt{90.92}$

sigma $= 9.54$

The negative signs prefacing certain values in the column headed "D" need not be shown since the further use of the negative values consists of squaring them, as may be noted in the column of Table XIII headed "D²." However, the negative sign is indispensable when checking calculations.

Computation of the Standard Deviation—Grouped Data

To illustrate the calculation of the standard deviation from grouped data, the distribution shown in Table XII is transferred to Table XIV. It requires one more column (fd^2) than was used to compute the mean from grouped data.

TABLE XIV

CALCULATION OF THE STANDARD DEVIATION FOR DATA SHOWN IN TABLE IV

ci	f	d	fd	fd^2
99-101	1	6	6	36
96- 98	3	5	15	75
93- 95	4	4	16	64
90- 92	5	3	15	45
87- 89	6	2	12	24
84- 86	8	1	8	8
81- 83	9	0	(+72)	0
78- 80	7	−1	−7	7
75- 77	6	−2	−12	24
72- 74	4	−3	−12	36
69- 71	4	−4	−16	64
66- 68	3	−5	−15	75
63- 65	0	−6	0	0
60- 62	1	−7	−7	49
			(−69)	
	$N = 61$		+3	507

$$SD = i\sqrt{\frac{\Sigma fd^2}{N} - c^2}$$

1. $SD = 3\sqrt{\dfrac{507}{61} - \left(\dfrac{3}{61}\right)^2}$

2. $SD = 3\sqrt{8.31147 - (.04918)^2}$

3. $SD = 3\sqrt{8.31147 - (.0492)^2}$

4. $SD = 3\sqrt{8.31147 - .00242}$

5. $SD = 3\sqrt{8.3115 - .0024}$

6. $SD = 3\sqrt{8.3091}$

7. $SD = 3 \times 2.88255$

8. $SD = 3 \times 2.8826$

9. $SD = 8.6478$

10. $SD = 8.65$

The formula for computing the standard deviation from an assumed mean in grouped data is:

$$\text{sigma} = i\sqrt{\frac{\Sigma fd^2}{N} - \left(\frac{\Sigma fd}{N}\right)^2} \quad \text{or } i\sqrt{\frac{\Sigma fd^2}{N} - c^2}.$$

The first seven steps listed under "Steps in Calculating the Mean— Grouped Data" are identical to the first seven steps used in finding standard deviation except for squaring the correction to the assumed mean. Additional steps required are as follows:

8. Square the correction to the assumed mean. The additional step is $(\Sigma fd/N)^2$ (or c^2) $= (3/61)^2 = .04918^2$ or .0024.

9. Complete the fd² column. This is done by multiplying the d value in each interval by the fd value for the same interval. The product is placed in the fd² column. For interval 99-101 the value is $6 \times 6 = 36$. The sum of the fd² values is 507. There are no negative values in this column.

10. Mean of the squared deviations of the scores. This is represented by the value $\Sigma fd^2/N$ which is 507/61 or 8.31147.

11. The corrected mean of the squared deviation of scores is

$$\sqrt{\Sigma fd^2/N - c^2} \text{ or } \sqrt{8.3115 - .0024} = \sqrt{8.3091}.$$

12. The standard deviation in terms of class intervals is

$$\sqrt{\Sigma fd^2/N - c^2} = \sqrt{8.3091} = 2.8826.$$

13. The standard deviation in terms of scale distance is

$i \sqrt{\Sigma fd^2/N - c^2}$ (i represents the size of the class interval)

or $i\sqrt{\Sigma fd^2/N - c^2} = 3 \times 2.8826 = 8.6478.$

14. Substitutions in the formula for sigma are shown in Table XIV. In some applications of sigma the final numerical values are represented as four digits beyond the decimal point (line 9), while in most of the applications in measurement two digits beyond the decimal point (line 10) are adequate.

Computing the Standard Deviation by the Raw Score Method

When the standard deviation is computed by the raw score method it is not necessary to obtain deviations from the mean or to set up a frequency distribution. It is a convenient method to use when a calculating machine is available or when there is not a large number of cases in ungrouped data. The formula is

$$\text{sigma} = \sqrt{\frac{\Sigma x^2}{N} - M^2}$$

If each of the 61 scores in Table IV were squared and the 61 squared values summated, the sum would be 415,826. The sum of 415,826 (Σx^2) divided by 61 (N) would equal 6816.820. The true mean of the scores in Table IV is 82.098 or 82.10. The mean squared is 6740.081. Substituting in the formula we have:

$$\text{Sigma} = \sqrt{\frac{415826}{61} - 6740.081}$$

$$= \sqrt{6816.820 - 6740.081}$$

$$= \sqrt{76.739}$$

$$= 8.760$$

Estimated Standard Deviation by Short Cut

A practical and fairly accurate estimate of standard deviation can be based on percentile points. The formula is sigma $= (P_{90} - P_{10}) \times 0.4$.

Probable Error as a Measure of Variability

Probable error is used to obtain an estimate of the dispersion or variability of a total population based on a random sample of that population. It is obtained by multiplying sigma by .6745. The range from one PE below ($-$ 1 PE) the mean to one PE above ($+$ 1 PE) the mean includes approximately the middle 50 percent of the cases or scores. If the distribution were symmetrical, we would not use the word "approximately." PE is used when in one situation we have the mean and PE and in another situation we have the median and Q (where such comparisons can be justified).

The sigma for the data in Table XIV is 8.6478. The probable error is $\sigma \times .6745$ or $(8.6478 \times .6745) = 5.83$.

Semi-Interquartile Range or Quartile Deviation (Q)

This measure of variability represents one-half the distance between Q_3 and Q_1 (P_{75} and P_{25}), and it is used in connection with the median of a total population or the actual scores. The distance from one Q below ($-$ 1 Q) the median to one Q above ($+$ 1 Q) the median includes approximately the middle 50 percent of the scores. The formula used is

$$Q = \frac{Q_3 - Q_1}{2}$$

Substituting the values obtained for our data in Table VI, we have

$$Q = \frac{88.38 - 76.13}{2} = 6.13$$

The discrepancy between Q and PE, while not significant, points out the factor of sensitivity of sigma (used in finding PE) to the nature of the distribution of scores in a frequency table. Quartile deviation is not based on deviation of scores from a specific average, and it is related indirectly to the form of the distribution of scores.

Average Deviation, Variance, and Range

Average deviation is a measure of variability obtained by finding the difference between each of the individual scores and the group average of the distribution, and averaging these differences regardless of their sign. It is a measure of variability based on the deviation of scores from the mean or median. In a skewed distribution, the deviation would be less from the median than from the mean. Apparently, comparatively little use has been made of average or mean deviation since 1925.

Variance is the standard deviation squared.

The *range* as a measure of variability is the difference between the lowest and highest scores in a distribution. The "total range," which is rarely used in measurements, is the difference between the lowest and highest scores plus one. It is affected by the fluctuation of scores at both ends of the distribution. The identity of the size of the smallest and largest scores is lost when only the range is expressed. Also, the range depends entirely on the two extreme score values with no indication as to the shape of the distribution.

GENERAL REFERENCES

Blommers, Paul and E. F. Lindquist: *Elementary Statistical Methods in Psychology and Education.* Boston, Houghton Mifflin, 1960, pp. 134-156.

Ferguson, Leonard W.: *Personality Measurement.* New York, McGraw-Hill, 1952, p. 61.

Freeman, Frank S.: *Theory and Practice of Psychological Testing,* 3rd ed. Chicago, Holt, Rinehart and Winston, 1962, pp. 30-33.

Greene, Harry A. *et al.*: *Measurement and Evaluation in the Elementary School,* 2nd ed. New York, Longmans, Green and Co., 1953, pp. 328-338.

Johnson, Palmer O. and Robert W. B. Jackson: *Introduction to Statistical Methods.* New York, Prentice-Hall, 1953, pp. 145-165.

Remmers, H. H. and N. L. Gage: *Educational Measurement and Evaluation,* Rev. ed. New York, Harper and Brothers, 1955, pp. 582-587.

Thorndike, Robert L. and Elizabeth Hagen: *Measurement and Evaluation in Psychology and Education,* 2nd ed. New York, John Wiley and Sons, 1961, pp. 109-116.

Van Dalen, Deobold B.: *Understanding Educational Research,* Enlarged and rev. ed. New York, McGraw-Hill, 1962, pp. 340-345.

7 STANDARD SCORES

Sᴛᴀɴᴅᴀʀᴅ scores are derived or transformed scores based on sigma units. Not all derived scores are standard scores. For example, the chronological age is not a derived value, but the mental age is a derived value. Raw scores on a test are comparatively meaningless except that they can be used to provide the relative standing of the individuals within a group. Standard scores are not only easily interpreted but they provide uniform ability increments for a given distribution or population. It is necessary, however, to assume that whatever trait that is measured represents a reasonably good normal distribution. Standard scores make it possible to express obtained scores on a uniformly calibrated standard scale (equal units) and still not change significantly the shape of the original distribution. The ordinary standard scores are based on the concept of nonlinear transformations and approximately normal curves.

COMPUTATION AND COMPARISON OF STANDARD SCORES

There are several different methods by which standard scores are computed and/or compared. The various approaches are illustrated here.

1. *Verbal Scores.* The simplest standard scores, also known as the standard deviation technique for assigning marks or placing persons into ability groups, are verbal scores. When verbal scores are used, the distribution is divided into five categories based upon the mean and sigma of the scores obtained by a given population. Following is an outline of the sigma values that are added to or subtracted from the mean to establish score limits for each verbal score.

For the sixty-one scores in Table IV, the mean is 82.15 (Table XII) and the sigma is 8.65 (Table XIV). Five-tenths of sigma is 4.33 and one and five-tenths of sigma is 12.98. Substituting in Table XV provides us with detailed information in Table XVI.

TABLE XV

SIGMA UNITS FOR VERBAL SCORES

Verbal Score	Computation Steps
1	$M + 1.5\sigma -$
II	$M + 0.5\sigma$ to $M + 1.5\sigma$
111	$M - 0.5\sigma$ to $M + 0.5\sigma$
IV	$M - 1.5\sigma$ to $M - 0.5\sigma$
V	$- M - 1.5\sigma$

The final form of the norm table or grade distribution table is shown in Table XVII. Verbal scores are placed in the second column and scores obtained (rounded limits) are placed in the first column to facilitate con-

TABLE XVI

SCORE LIMITS, TABULATIONS AND FREQUENCIES FOR THE SCORES IN TABLE IV

Verbal Score	Fractional Limits	*Rounded Limits	Tabulations	f
I	95.13-	96-	/ / / /	4
II	86.48-95.13	87-95	-/-/-/-/- -/-/-/-/- -/-/-/-/-	15
III	77.82-86.48	78-86	-/-/-/-/- -/-/-/-/- -/-/-/-/- -/-/-/-/- / / / /	24
IV	69.17-77.82	70-77	-/-/-/-/- -/-/-/-/- / /	12
V	-69.17	-69	-/-/-/-/- /	6

verting the scores. The verbal score categories are sometimes called ability groups. A verbal score of I would indicate superior ability; II, above average; III, average; IV, below average; and V, academic risk.

TABLE XVII

SCORE LIMITS FOR VERBAL SCORES BASED ON SCORES IN TABLE IV

Score Interval	Verbal Score
96-	I
87-95	II
78-86	III
70-77	IV
-69	V

For verbal scores the mean is III and the sigma is one. There are four points and five areas or categories in the verbal score distribution.

2. *Stanine Scores.* During World War II, the U. S. Navy made use of the five ability groups described above as well as other derived scores. The Army Air Force introduced stanine scores which provide for nine ability groups. The mean is 5 and the standard deviation is 2. (See Appendix A.

*For rounding see discussion following Table VIII.

Stanine 5 is at σ value 0.0 and 7 is at σ value 1.0. The distance from stanine 5 to stanine 7 is 2.) Stanines are represented as single digit standard scores.

The procedure used to set up stanine tables is similar to that used in connection with verbal scores. Sigma values that are added to or subtracted from the mean are shown in Table XVIII.

TABLE XVIII

SIGMA LIMITS FOR STANINE SCORES

Stanine	Computation Steps
9	$M + 1.75\sigma -$
8	$M + 1.25\sigma$ to $M + 1.75\sigma$
7	$M + 0.75\sigma$ to $M + 1.25\sigma$
6	$M + 0.25\sigma$ to $M + 0.75\sigma$
5	$M - 0.25\sigma$ to $M + 0.25\sigma$
4	$M - 0.75\sigma$ to $M - 0.25\sigma$
3	$M - 1.25\sigma$ to $M - 0.75\sigma$
2	$M - 1.75\sigma$ to $M - 1.25\sigma$
1	$- M - 1.75\sigma$

To arrive at the intervals for each stanine value we will again use the mean (82.15) and the sigma (8.65) used in the illustration for verbal scores. The sigma values are $0.25 \times 8.65 = 2.16$, $0.75 \times 8.65 = 6.49$, $1.25 \times 8.65 = 10.81$, and $1.75 \times 8.65 = 15.14$. Substituting these values in Table XVIII provides the basis for the detailed information in Table XIX.

TABLE XIX

SCORE LIMITS, TABULATIONS, AND FREQUENCIES FOR THE SCORES IN TABLE IV

Stanine	Fractional Limits	Rounded Limits	Tabulations	f
9	97.29-	98-	/ /	2
8	92.96-97.29	93-97	-/-/-/-/- /	6
7	88.64-92.96	89-92	-/-/-/-/- / /	7
6	84.31-88.64	85-88	-/-/-/-/- -/-/-/-/-	10
5	79.99-84.31	80-84	-/-/-/-/- -/-/-/-/- / / /	13
4	75.66-79.99	76-79	-/-/-/-/- / / / /	9
3	71.34-75.66	72-75	-/-/-/-/- /	6
2	67.01-71.34	68-71	-/-/-/-/-	5
1	-67.01	-67	/ / /	3

The procedure used to convert scores to stanines is shown in Table XX. It is well to show the score interval in the first column as it is the score obtained or to be converted that is brought to the norm or conversion table. Hence the convenience of entering the first column.

TABLE XX

SCORE LIMITS FOR STANINES BASED ON THE SCORES IN TABLE IV

Score Interval	Stanine
98-	9
93-97	8
89-92	7
85-88	6
80-84	5
76-79	4
72-75	3
68-71	2
-67	1

3. *The z-score.* The z-score is a standard score usually indicated as z. The mean is 0.0 and the sigma is 1, with the unit of measurement designated as one-tenth of sigma (see Appendix A, column 1). In measurements the range from —3.0 to +3.0σ is considered quite functional. On occasion the range is extended over a distance of 10 sigmas. The formula for converting raw scores to z-scores is $z = (X — M)/\sigma$, where X is any score in the distribution, M is the mean of the distribution, and σ is the standard deviation of the distribution. The mean for our data in Table IV is 82.15 (Table XII) and the sigma is 8.65 (Table XIV). If we use the score 72 from Table IV and substitute the values in the formula, it would appear as $z = (72 — 82.15)/8.65 = —10.15/8.65 = —1.17$ or —1.2. To avoid negative values and decimal points the z-score is multiplied by 10 and the mean designated as 50. It is then more properly called a Z-score.

This procedure for finding the standard score is sometimes confused with a normalized standard score which has a mean of 50 and a sigma of 10. It is a T-score. Ebel's[13] suggestion of designating the standard score as a Z-score would avoid the confusion. The standard score as previously stated does not alter the original shape of the distribution, except for a very minor change due to grouping error. The T-score, a normalized standard score, uses as its point of departure percentile norms (see Appendix A).

4. *Other Typical Standard Scores.* There are several standard score systems currently in use with a variation in means and sigmas but each one has a similar relationship to the symmetrical normal curve. Examples of standard scores with varied means and sigmas in common use are: (1) Army General Classification Test—M = 100, Sigma = 20; (2) Navy

13. Ebel, Robert E.: *Measuring Educational Achievement.* Englewood Cliffs, New Jersey, Prentice-Hall, 1965, p. 469.

Standard Score—M = 50, sigma = 10; (3) College Boards—M = 500, sigma = 100; and (4) all ETS Subject Examinations—M = 50, sigma = 10, etc. It becomes obvious that the standard scores listed are based on the z-score method but different constants are used. A chart devised by the Psychological Corporation[14] in 1955 shows the relationships among several standard scores. See also the chart in Appendix B.

5. *Deviation IQ as a Standard Score.* There is a trend toward using standard scores for interpreting the results of both scholastic aptitude and achievement tests. The only real resemblance of a true DIQ to the ratio IQ, as originally proposed by Stern, is in the letters "I" and "Q." The IQ part of the designation causes less confusion (during a transition period) in interpreting an examinee's general ability. Goodenough[15] has suggested that the term "IQ Equivalent" be used to avoid confusion. A mean of 100 and a sigma of 16 provides a reasonably close resemblance to the previously recognized distribution of intelligence quotients in a representative population. The sigma value could of course be increased or decreased. The T-score method results in equal DIQs at all age levels, except for error of measurement and change in intellectual level to perform.

The 1960 revision of the Stanford-Binet Intelligence Scale by Terman and Merrill provides for IQ norms that have basically a mean of 100 and a sigma of 16. The revised (1966) *Pintner-Cunningham Primary Test-Pintner General Alibity Tests*[16] makes use of normalized standard scores with a mean of 100 and a standard deviation of 16.

NORMALIZED STANDARD SCORES

Normalized standard scores may at first glance appear to be the same as the derived scores called standard scores. There is a difference in that they are based on nonlinear transformations. It is necessary to set up percentile ranks (or norms) as illustrated in Table X. The distribution of scores is drawn out or extended over a scale that includes percentile values from approximately 1 through 99 for a given set of test scores and group (or normative population). We should assume that the distribution of raw scores upon which the percentiles are based is approximately normal. It should be recognized that the characteristics of the test that could result from the nature of con-

14. *Test Service Bulletin* 48, The Psychological Corporation, January, 1955.
15. Goodenough, Florence L.: *Mental Testing.* New York, Rinehart and Company, 1949, p. 199.
16. Pintner, Rudolf, Bess V. Cunningham, Walter N. Durost: *Pintner-Cunningham Primary Tests, Pintner General Ability Test.* New York, Harcourt, Brace and World, 1966.

struction may influence considerably the shape of the distribution of obtained scores. However, test score distributions tend to resemble the normal curve. For the kind of sampling (large and representative) that is used when standardized tests are developed, there is little reason to doubt the normality of the distribution. Under those conditions the discrepancy between standard scores and normalized scores is relatively insignificant. When the distribution of raw scores departs from the normal curve it is better to use the linearly derived standard scores.

With the completion of the percentile distribution or percentile norm table, it is almost a mechanical procedure to obtain the normalized standard scores. Such scores can be read from a table, such as the table in Appendix A, using the percentile column as the point of departure. To illustrate the procedure we will refer to Table X and use a raw score of 94. The percentile rank of the score 94 is 90. The PR of 90 is 1.3 sigmas above the mean (see column 1, Appendix A), which is identically the same as a z-score of 1.3. To convert the z-score to a normalized T-score, the z-score is multiplied by 10, the product is algebraically added to 50, which results in $1.3 \times 10 + 50 = 63$. The normalized T-score then is 63, which is the same as the score to the left of the PR 90 in column 5.

Should we desire, for example, to transform the z-score value of 1.3 to a CEEB score ($M = 500$, $\sigma = 100$) we would use the following steps: $1.3 \times 100 + 500 = 630$.

By referring to Appendix A, we can transform a PR of 90 to a T-score (column 5) of 63, a stanine score of 8 (column 3), and a verbal score of II (column 2).

Normalized standard scores have certain computational advantages. For example, when we use normalized standard scores, we are dealing with equal units on a scale while in the case of percentiles, we do not have such equal units. However, percentile scores are readily meaningful when interpreting test results. Normalized standard scores make it possible to compare the scores on different tests. As previously indicated, ordinary standard scores assume the shape of the original distribution from which they were obtained.

GENERAL REFERENCES

Blommers, Paul and E. F. Lindquist: *Elementary Statistical Methods in Psychology and Education.* Boston, Houghton Mifflin, 1960, pp. 157-176.

Cronbach, Lee J.: *Essentials of Psychological Testing,* 2nd ed. New York, Harper and Brothers, 1960, pp. 78-85.

Ferguson, Leonard W.: *Personality Measurement.* New York, McGraw-Hill, 1952, pp. 262-266.

Freeman, Frank S.: *Theory and Practice of Psychological Testing,* 3rd ed. Chicago, Holt, Rinehart and Winston, 1962, pp. 128-134.

Goodenough, Florence L.: *Mental Testing.* New York, Rinehart and Company, 1949, pp. 189-200.

Remmers, H. H. and N. L. Gage: *Educational Measurement and Evaluation,* Rev. ed. New York, Harper and Brothers, 1956, pp. 589-593.

Thorndike, Robert L. and Elizabeth Hagen: *Measurement and Evaluation in Psychology and Education,* 2nd ed. New York, John Wiley and Sons, 1961, pp. 137-144.

Tiedeman, David V.: "Has He Grown?" *Test Service Notebook,* No. 12. New York, World Book Company.

Van Dalen, Deobold B.: *Understanding Educational Research,* Enlarged and rev. ed. New York, McGraw-Hill, 1962, pp. 345-352.

8 GRAPHICAL REPRESENTATIONS OF DATA

T HE graphical representations referred to in this discussion pertain largely to the recording and interpretation of test scores. They do not include the recording of ideas by means of symbols other than numerical values. In psychological measurement the graphic representation should show clearly or describe vividly the data which it represents.

The basic assumptions regarding the distribution of scores within the class intervals is not the same when constructing histograms and frequency polygons. It is assumed that the scores are uniformly distributed in the histogram and that they lie at the midpoint of the interval in the frequency polygon.

A guideline to the construction of graphical representations might well be the accuracy or the extent to which the original data can be reconstructed from the graphic representation. To keep this in mind oftentimes helps in the construction of the graphic representation. The method of graphic representation used should be such that it makes observations and interpretations reasonably accurate and efficient.

THE HISTOGRAM

Bar diagrams and histograms frequently are confused. A bar diagram has space between each of the rectangles or bars all of which are the same width but of varying lengths. A histogram is a graphic representation of a frequency distribution. The frequencies are represented as areas by means of rectangles all of which are the same width representing the size of the class interval. The length of the rectangles is proportionate to the number of frequencies in the interval. There is no space between the rectangles and they should not be made into pictographs or decorated to improve their appearance. Bar diagrams place the emphasis on separate bars of different lengths. These characteristics distinguish the histogram from the bar diagram.

Use and Construction of the Histogram

The histogram makes it possible to observe more clearly the main characteristics of the frequency distribution. Each base of a column represents the range of the interval or the size of the class interval with its limits. The height of each column represents the number of frequencies in the interval. A clearer representation of data can usually be obtained if the histogram is a little wider than it is tall and these dimensions also tend to avoid the impression of distortion which is sometimes created by poorly constructed histograms or frequency polygons.

Steps to use in constructing a histogram:

1. Make two straight lines that form a right angle in the lower left corner to establish the left and lower edges of the histogram.

2. Lay off in equal-length units at the lower edge the lower limits of the class intervals. Start just to the right of each lower limit to establish and write in the lower limit numerical value, from left to right. This is indicated by the numerical value of 60 in Figure 2. Notice that the last value in Figure 2 is 102 which would be the lower limit of the next higher interval if there were one. Leave space on the base line at the right hand end which is the equivalent of one-half an interval.

3. Show frequency points and values. Lay off on the left side line equal units of distance to show the number of frequencies in each class interval. The length of each unit should be such that it will make a well proportioned histogram. Indicate the frequency value just above the points established while laying out the equal distances. Remember to start with zero frequency and move up the scale to equal or preferably to go a little beyond the largest number of frequencies in any one interval. The frequency values may be shown in terms of a multiple of 2 or a larger number but the lowest value must always be zero.

4. Complete the upper and right side margins of the histogram. Leave space between the highest frequency rectangle in terms of score intervals and the right side of the histogram. See Figure 2.

5. Rule in the rectangles. The top edge of each rectangle shows the number of frequencies and the lower end shows the limits of the class interval. The limits are from the lower limit *to* the lower limit of the next higher interval. Zero frequencies should be shown by means of a slightly heavier line as shown in Figure 2 for interval 63 *to* interval 66.

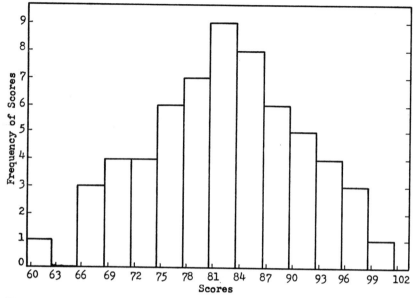

Figure 2. Histogram representing the sixty-one scores shown in Table V.

USE AND CONSTRUCTION OF THE FREQUENCY POLYGON

The frequency polygon is more useful when one wishes to superimpose two or more frequency distributions. It is quite effective in showing the characteristics of the frequency distribution. The frequency polygon lends itself well to situations where one wishes to show the continuity of data. In most of the work with psychological measurement we are not dealing with discrete data.

Steps in the procedure of constructing a frequency polygon:

1. Establish the left and lower edges of the frequency polygon. Follow the procedure used in step one under constructing the histogram.

2. Lay off equal-length units at the lower edge to represent the *midpoints* of the class intervals. It is necessary to establish an additional equal-length unit at both the left and right end of the lower edge or base line. These equal-length units represent the upper and lower limits of the class intervals. Next, establish the midpoints of the intervals on the base line and record the numerical values of the midpoints.

3. To establish the frequency points and values and the upper and right side margins follow steps 3 and 4 above for constructing the histogram.

4. Establish points to be connected by straight lines. Directly above the

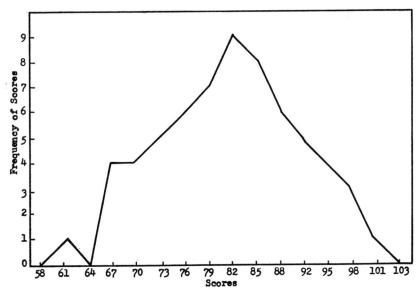

Figure 3. Frequency polygon representing the sixty-one scores shown in Table V.

midpoint of each interval place a point that lies to the right of the frequencies for each interval.

5. Final step to complete the graphic representation. Connect the points established in step 4. The connecting lines must be brought down to the base line to show zero frequencies. Theoretically the lines should not quite reach the base line.

Figure 3 shows a completed frequency polygon for the 61 scores shown in Table V. For the purpose of further clarification compare Illustration 1 with Figure 3. Note particularly the midpoint values at the lower (midpoint 58) and upper end (midpoint 103) of the frequency polygon. These midpoints lie in the intervals referred to as the equal-length units at the left and right end of the base line.

A simplified illustration is provided by the information in Illustration 1. The broken lines represent the histogram and the solid line represents the frequency polygon. The midpoints of the intervals are shown in their proper position while the lower limits of the class intervals are dropped down below their normal position.

USE AND CONSTRUCTION OF THE OGIVE CURVE

The ogive curve is the familiar "S" curve frequently used in intro-

Illustration 1

Data Represented by a Frequency Distribution and How a
Frequency Polygon is Related to the Histogram

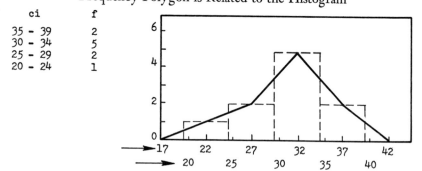

ci	f
35 - 39	2
30 - 34	5
25 - 29	2
20 - 24	1

ductory courses in psychology. This serviceable representation of a
distribution of scores is also called a cumulative frequency curve or
cumulative frequency graph. It is not necessary to calculate percentages to construct the cumulative frequency curve nor is it implied in its title that it be done.

The ogive curve, since it is based on cumulative frequencies, tends
to smooth irregularities. Percentile values (quartiles, etc.) can be
estimated quite readily as well as the percentile rank of a given score
(see percentile curve). By modifying the data portion of the ogive
curve work sheet, it is possible to superimpose two or more X grades
or grade X with all X grades combined for the school system.

The accuracy of placing points to form the curve depends upon the
number of cases, the size and number of class intervals, and the precision with which the graph is made. Figure 4 contains the data
used and the resulting ogive curve. It should be noted that the same
rules of thumb are used that were used in setting up the frequency
distribution in Chapter 3. The height of the curve should be at least
that of the number of class intervals shown. It is desirable to have
the curve one or two intervals taller. This facilitates the accuracy
with which percentiles and score values can be estimated.

The following steps are an aid in the construction of an ogive
curve.

1. Set up a frequency distribution as was done in constructing Table V.

2. The width of the ogive curve is determined by the number of class
intervals and the distance allowed between interval limits. Establish the

equal distance units on the base line. Show the integral lower limits of the class intervals just to the right of the point that represents the lower limit of each interval. Keep in mind that in our calculations we use fractional limits, as fractional limits are real limits in psychological data.

3. Complete the cf scale. The unit used may be an odd or even value. Select a unit that will make the height of the cf scale at least as tall or preferably two or three units higher to facilitate ease of interpretation. In Figure 4 a unit of 4 or multiple of 4 is used to designate the values on the cf scale.

4. Complete graph layout and its margins as illustrated in Figure 4.

5. Establish points on the perpendicular at the end of each class interval unit. The height of each point is determined by the number of scores that have been accumulated at the end of the class interval designated on the base line. The beginning of the curve must lie at the zero point of the cf scale. One score has accumulated in the interval 60-62 therefore a point is placed one-fourth of the distance, just to the left of the 63 on the base line, up to the cf scale value 4. Since there are no frequencies in the interval 63-65 a point is placed one-fourth of the distance, just to the left of the 66 on the base line, up to the cf scale value 4. Four scores have accumulated through the interval 66-68, consequently a point is placed directly opposite the cf scale value 4 and just to the left and above the 69 on the base line. Proceed in this manner until all 15 points have been established.

6. Complete the ogive (or cumulative frequency) curve by starting at the zero point and connecting the 15 points.

7. Estimate percentile values. In Figure 4 we will estimate quartiles. Divide the perpendicular above 102 to the point of intersection with the ogive curve into four equal parts. The four parts or units are of equal lengths and the three points (Q_3, Mdn, and Q_1) show the limits of each of the four parts. Extend a broken line from Q_3 (parallel to the base line) to the ogive curve and at the point of intersection drop a perpendicular (broken line) to the base line. Estimate by interpolation the score value at the base line which for Q_3 is approximately 88. Use the same procedure to estimate the score values for the median and Q_1.

By starting with a score value on the base line it is possible to estimate the quartile rank of a given score in the distribution. Quintile and decile points and quintile and decile ranks may likewise be estimated.

USE AND CONSTRUCTION OF THE PERCENTILE CURVE

It may be noted that the percentile curve, also known as the percentile graph, which is shown in Figure 5 is an inverted "S" curve.

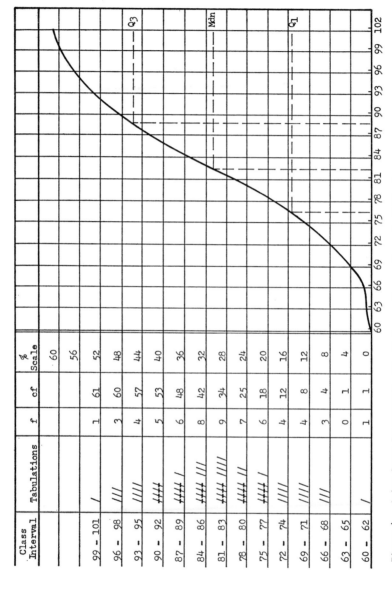

Class Interval	Tabulations	f	cf	% Scale
				60
				56
99 - 101	/	1	61	52
96 - 98	///	3	60	48
93 - 95	////	4	57	44
90 - 92	++++	5	53	40
87 - 89	++++ /	6	48	36
84 - 86	++++ ///	8	42	32
81 - 83	++++ ////	9	34	28
78 - 80	++++ //	7	25	24
75 - 77	++++ /	6	18	20
72 - 74	////	4	12	16
69 - 71	////	4	8	12
66 - 68	///	3	4	8
63 - 65		0	1	4
60 - 62	/	1	1	0

Figure 4. Ogive Curve Representing the Sixty-one Scores Shown in Table 5.

Compare the shape of the curve in Figure 5 with the shape of the curve shown in Figure 4. The use and applications of the percentile curve are similar to the ogive curve. The construction of the ogive curve is based on cumulative frequencies while the percentile curve is based on cumulative percents. It is a convenient device for estimating the percentile ranks of scores. If the point of departure is from the base line, quarters can be quite readily estimated.

There are several steps in the procedure of setting up a percentile curve that need to be recognized.

1. Lay out a chart similar to Figure 5.

2. Complete the class interval column, tabulations, frequency, and cumulative frequency columns.

3. Calculate the cumulative percent (cum %) values. In figure 5 the cf value for each interval is divided by 61 (N). The quotient is carried to four digits beyond the decimal point with no rounding. Some persons carry the division to three digits beyond the decimal point and round on the nearest whole number.

4. Establish equal length units on the base line of the grid (see Figure 5) to be used for erecting perpendiculars to locate points that represent score values between the horizontal lines. The horizontal lines are in reality an extension of the horizontal lines used to set up the frequency distribution and the perpendiculars are a series of points on the horizontal lines. The base line will show 10 scale units and 11 points, 0 to 100. This will then represent all percentages of cases, from 0 to 100, that are in a given distribution. The height of the percentile curve is the same as the upper limit of the top class interval.

5. Establish the points to be used in constructing the percentile curve. The first point must be established at the 0 percentile value. The second point is placed on the horizontal line representing the upper limit of interval 60-62 and the lower limit of interval 63-65. This point represents the percent of scores that have accumulated through the interval 60-62, hence the point is estimated to be about 1.6 the distance from 0 to 10. Since there are no frequencies in the interval 63-65, we still have only 1.6 percent of the cases accumulated so that the point is placed directly above the point for interval 60-62. Through the interval 66-68 a total of 6.6 percent of the cases have accumulated hence the fourth point is placed approximately 6.6 the distance from 0 to 10 on the base line. To illustrate further, through the interval 69-71 a total of 13.1 percent of the cases have accumulated so the fifth point is placed approximately 3.1 the distance from 10 to 20 (indicated on the base line) on the horizontal line

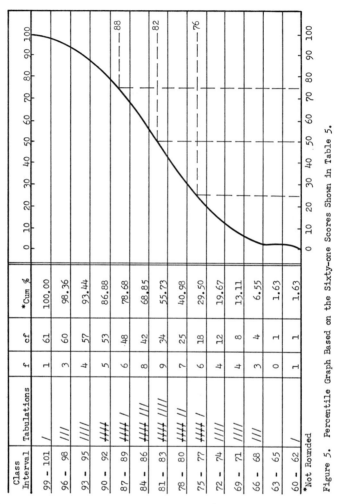

Class Interval	Tabulations	f	cf	*Cum %
99 - 101	/	1	61	100.00
96 - 98	///	3	60	98.36
93 - 95	////	4	57	93.44
90 - 92	////	5	53	86.88
87 - 89	//// /	6	48	78.68
84 - 86	//// ///	8	42	68.85
81 - 83	//// ////	9	34	55.73
78 - 80	//// //	7	25	40.98
75 - 77	//// /	6	18	29.50
72 - 74	////	4	12	19.67
69 - 71	////	4	8	13.11
66 - 68	///	3	4	6.55
63 - 65		0	1	1.63
60 - 62	/	1	1	1.63

*Not Rounded

Figure 5. Percentile Graph Based on the Sixty-one Scores Shown in Table 5.

which represents the upper limit of the class interval 69-71. Complete the establishment of the remaining points using the above procedure. The last point established will be on the horizontal line representing the upper limit of the interval 99-101 and directly above the 100 percentile value on the base line.

6. Establish the percentile curve by connecting the points 0 to 100 by means of smoothed or curved lines.

7. Estimate score values for certain percentile points.

The percentile graph is a convenient technique for estimating the score values for percentile ranks. If we were to estimate quartiles, we would proceed by erecting a perpendicular (broken line, as solid lines tend to clutter the graphic representation) from a point midway between the percentile values of 20 and 30 on the base line up to the percentile curve. At the point of intersection with the curve, the broken line would be extended to the right, parallel with the horizontal lines that represent limits of the class intervals, to the perpendicular above the 100 percentile on the base line. The 25th percentile or Q_1 would be about 76. The median and Q_3 are arrived at in the same manner. Other percentile values, as indicated for the ogive curve, may also be estimated. The procedure may be reversed and the percentile rank for any given score in the distribution may be estimated.

Graphic representations are useful aids when obtained scores are interpreted in terms of their relationship to a given population. It is a meaningful way to show pupils or counselees their level of accomplishment on certain tests.

GENERAL REFERENCES

Garrett, Henry E.: *Elementary Statistics*. New York, Longmans, Green and Co., 1956, pp. 19-26.

Greene, Harry A. *et al.*: *Measurement and Evaluation in the Elementary School*. New York, Longmans, Green and Co., 1953, pp. 355-363.

McCall, William A.: *Measurement*. New York, Macmillan, 1939, pp. 473-492.

Noll, Victor H.: *Introduction to Educational Measurement*. Boston, Houghton Mifflin, 1957, pp. 403-406.

Remmers, H. H. and N. L. Gage: *Educational Measurement and Evaluation*, Rev. ed. New York, Harper and Brothers, 1955, pp. 576-578.

Ross, C. C. and Julian C. Stanley: *Measurement in Today's Schools*, 3rd ed. New York, Prentice-Hall, 1954, pp. 247-273.

Thorndike, Robert L. and Elizabeth Hagen: *Measurement and Evaluation in Psychology and Education*, 2nd ed. New York, John Wiley and Sons, Inc., 1961, pp. 147-153.

Traxler, Arthur E., Robert Jacobs, Margaret Selover and Agatha Townsend: *Introduction to Testing and the Use of Test Results in Public Schools*. New York, Harper and Brothers, pp. 80-87.

Wrightstone, J. Wayne, Joseph Justman and Irving Robbins: *Evaluation in Modern Education*. New York, American, 1956, pp. 449-450.

9 CORRELATION IN PSYCHOLOGICAL MEASUREMENT

T EST construction, validation, selection, and the use and interpretation of the results obtained from measuring instruments, make it imperative that we recognize the function of correlation. Correlation represents the degree of relationship or the "co-relation" between two (or more) variables. This relationship is commonly expressed by a coefficient of correlation. Basically it is a procedure involving comparisons. For example, we may compare the score obtained by each individual in a group of persons on a scholastic aptitude test with the score obtained on a subtest (or total score) of an achievement test battery. The phase of the correlation concept introduced at this point is based on the assumption that the score values with which we are concerned represent approximately normal distributions.

At this level in measurement the use of correlation coefficients pertains mainly to the areas of validity and reliability of tests. Another very important application of the coefficient of correlation is in making predictions. It should be noted that much of the confidence that we can place in predictions depends upon the amount and accuracy as well as the validity of the information upon which the predictions are based.

The first significant published study in which specific correlation coefficients were based on a mathematical formula (Karl Pearson formula) was done by Clark Wissler[17] in 1901. He summarized the results of his study by listing 42 Pearson r's.

17. Wissler, Clark: "The Correlation of Physical and Mental Tests," *The Psychological Review*. Edited by J. Mark Baldwin, J. McKeen Cattell, and W. C. Warren, Series of Monograph Supplements, Volume III, Number 6 (whole number 16), June, 1901.

Correlation procedures before the time of Sir Francis Galton were comparatively crude and resembled what is now called an expectancy grid or scatter diagram. At that time the expressions used were largely "inverse" and "direct" relationships or co-relations as used by Galton. The terms are as appropriate today as they were in the days of Sir Francis Galton. In addition to those terms we have precise quantitative values to express correlation.

Karl Pearson who was familiar with the correlation concept used by Bravais modified it and developed the mathematical procedures for the Pearson method or the Pearson Product-moment formula. It is based on the divergence of scores from the mean. The correlation (r) obtained by using his formula is frequently called the *Pearsonian r*.

C. W. Spearman contributed two relatively simple formulas based on ranking of scores. The "rank method" or "rank-difference method" (also called Spearman Rank-Difference Method) is used in situations where the sample is relatively small or when ratings are used. The formula is

$$\text{rho} = 1 - \frac{6\Sigma D^2}{N(N^2 - 1)}$$

His Foot Rule

$$R = 1 - \frac{6\Sigma G}{N^2 - 1}$$

is also based on ranking of scores. It is a shorter method and at best only a rough estimate of correlation as will be illustrated later.

When fewer than 15 cases are involved, the correlation should be considered with caution. Rho may be estimated quite conveniently when 15 to 30 or even a few more cases are considered. The application of several adaptations of the Pearson method and the rank-difference method are illustrated in the following pages, all of which are based on the same 29 cases. Without the use of electronic calculations, the arithmetic involved becomes quite extensive, especially when as many as 75 or more cases are involved. The use of the scatter diagram (or scattergram) as a point of departure when calculating the Pearsonian r can be quite convenient.

The vertical distribution of intervals in Illustrations 2 through 4 represent the Y-axis scores (any subject or variable, for convenience we will say Test Y) and the horizontal intervals represent the frequency distribution of the X-axis scores (we will call Test X). The

Scatter Diagrams of Cases Selected from Table XXI

Illustration 2

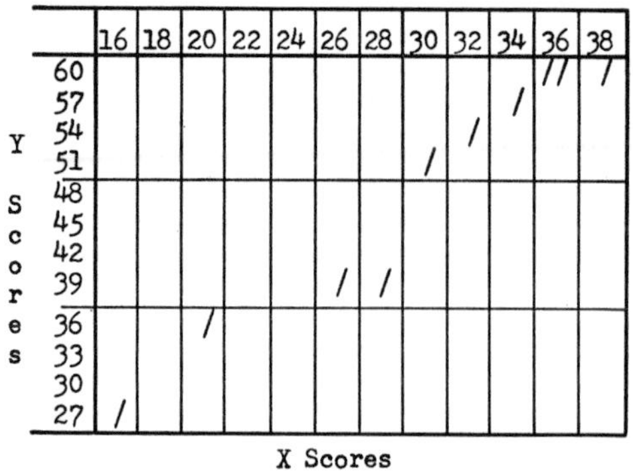

(r = .747)

X Scores

Illustration 3

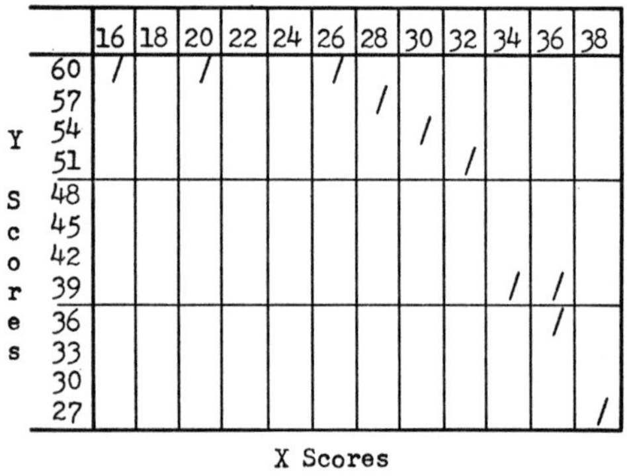

(r = − .830)

X Scores

Illustration 4

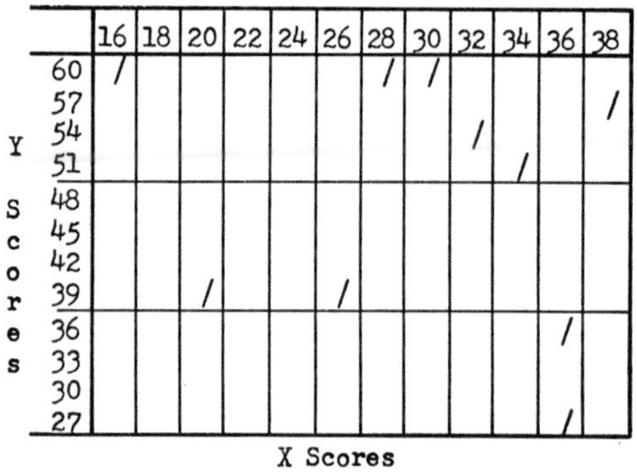

(r = .157)

X Scores

double-entry table or scatter diagram has the scores tabulated at points of intersection. For example, a person obtaining a score of 38 on Test X and 60 on Test Y would have his scores represented by a tally mark in the top row and the right hand column. If he obtained a score of 16 or 17 on Test X and score of 27 or 28 on Test Y, the tally mark representing the two scores would be placed in the first column and in the bottom row of Illustration 2. To the extent that scores cluster along a diagonal line from lower left to upper right of the scatter diagram we approach a higher positive correlation (Illus. 2); if the scores cluster along an upper left and lower right diagonal, we approach a high negative correlation (Illus. 3); and if there is a general scatterization of scores, we approach a zero correlation (Illus. 4).

The basic formula devised by Pearson is

$$r = \frac{\Sigma xy}{\sqrt{\Sigma x^2 \Sigma y^2}}$$

which may also be written as

$$r = \frac{\Sigma xy}{N \sigma_x \sigma_y}$$

There are other adaptations of the product-moment method depending somewhat on the facilities available as well as personal preferences.

The scores used to illustrate the application of correlation formulas shown by the data in Tables XXI-XXVII are the same for each of the seven tables. The data consist of raw scores obtained by students on two different reading tests. The X-axis represents scores obtained on the "H" Reading Test, and the Y-axis represents scores obtained on the "SA" Reading Test by 29 students. The N when used in a formula refers to the number of pairs of scores or students.

The steps for calculating r using the formula

$$r = \frac{\Sigma xy}{\sqrt{\Sigma x^2 \Sigma y^2}}$$

as shown in Table XXI follow:

1. In column 1 enter the number or name of the subjects and in columns 2 and 3 enter the pairs of scores for each subject.

2. Find the mean of the scores in column 2: 25.931 and column 3: 42.724.

TABLE XXI

CALCULATION FOR R USING THE FORMULA
DERIVED BY KARL PEARSON

1 Subj.	2 Sc X	3 Sc Y	4 x	5 y	6 x^2	7 y^2	8 xy
1	34	55	8.069	12.276	65.109	150.700	99.055
2	16	28	− 9.931	−14.724	98.625	216.796	146.224
3	36	61	10.069	18.276	101.385	334.012	184.021
4	31	39	5.069	− 3.724	25.695	13.868	− 18.877
5	27	38	1.069	− 4.724	1.143	22.316	− 5.050
6	29	51	3.069	8.276	9.419	68.492	25.399
7	36	59	10.069	16.276	101.385	264.908	163.883
8	38	61	12.069	18.276	145.661	334.012	220.573
9	33	61	7.069	18.276	49.971	334.012	129.193
10	20	39	− 5.931	− 3.724	35.177	13.868	22.087
11	11	34	−14.931	− 8.724	222.935	76.108	130.258
12	15	32	−10.931	−10.724	119.487	115.004	117.224
13	28	38	2.069	− 4.724	4.281	22.316	− 9.774
14	38	55	12.069	12.276	145.661	150.700	148.159
15	25	46	− 0.931	3.276	0.867	10.732	− 3.050
16	25	43	− 0.931	0.276	0.867	0.076	− 0.257
17	20	22	− 5.931	−20.724	35.177	429.484	122.914
18	14	25	−11.931	−17.724	142.349	314.140	211.465
19	19	35	− 6.931	− 7.724	48.039	59.660	53.535
20	35	54	9.069	11.276	82.247	127.148	102.262
21	32	43	6.069	0.276	36.833	0.076	1.675
22	32	49	6.069	6.276	36.833	39.388	38.089
23	18	25	− 7.931	−17.724	62.901	314.140	140.569
24	13	19	−12.931	−23.724	167.211	562.828	306.775
25	27	40	1.069	− 2.724	1.143	7.420	− 2.912
26	17	43	− 8.931	0.276	79.763	0.076	− 2.465
27	32	45	6.069	2.276	36.833	5.180	13.813
28	28	53	2.069	10.276	4.281	105.596	21.261
29	23	46	− 2.931	3.276	8.591	10.732	− 9.602

T = 752   1239   1869.869   4103.788   2346.447
M = 25.931 42.724   64.478   141.510

$$r = \frac{\Sigma xy}{\sqrt{\Sigma x^2 \Sigma y^2}}$$

$$r = \frac{2346.447}{\sqrt{1869.869 \times 4103.788}}$$

$$r = \frac{2346.447}{\sqrt{7673545.964}}$$

$$r = \frac{2346.477}{2770.177}$$

$$r = .847$$

3. In column 4 enter the difference between each X score and the mean of the X scores. In column 5 show the difference between each Y score and the mean of the Y scores.

4. Square each x value and enter it in column 6. Square each y value and enter it in column 7.

5. For each subject find the product of the x and y values (columns 4 and 5) and enter the product in column 8.

6. Find the sum of the x^2, y^2, and xy values (columns 6, 7, and 8).

7. Substitute the numerical values in the formula for r.

8. Divide the Σxy by the square root of the Σx^2 times Σy^2.

9. The steps are shown in detail in Table XXI where the correlation equals .847.

Steps for computing r when the formula used is

$$r = \frac{\Sigma xy}{N\sigma_x\sigma_y}$$

as shown in Table XXII are as follows:

1. Enter the name or number of the subjects in column 1. In columns 2 and 3 enter the pairs of scores for each subject.

2. Find the mean of the scores in columns 2 and 3 which are 25.931 and 42.724 respectively.

3. In column 4 enter the difference between each X score and the mean of the X scores. Enter the difference between each Y score and the mean of the Y scores in column 5.

4. Square each x value (column 4) and enter it in column 6. Square each y value (column 5) and enter it in column 7.

5. Find the product of the x and y values (columns 4 and 5) and enter the product in column 8.

6. Obtain the sums of the x^2 (1869.869), y^2 (4103.788) and xy values (2346.447) and enter in columns 6, 7 and 8.

7. To obtain σ_x and σ_y it is necessary to calculate first the mean of the

$$x^2 \left(\frac{\Sigma x^2}{N} = 64.478 \right) \text{ and } y^2 \left(\frac{\Sigma y^2}{N} = 141.510 \right) \text{ values}$$

8. To find the denominator of the basic formula it is necessary to take

$$29 \times \sqrt{64.478 \times 141.510} \text{ or } 29 \times \sqrt{9124.282}$$

which equals 29×95.521 or 2770.109.

9. Substitute the above numerical values in the formula

$$r = \frac{\Sigma xy}{N\sigma_x\sigma_y}$$

10. The steps used in making the substitutions in the formula are shown by the data in Table XXII where the $r = .847$.

TABLE XXII

CALCULATION OF r USING THE PEARSON FORMULA EXPRESSED AS

$$r = \frac{\Sigma xy}{N\sigma_x\sigma_y}$$

1	2	3	4	5	6	7	8
Subj.	Sc X	Sc Y	x	y	x^2	y^2	xy
1	34	55	8.069	12.276	65.109	150.700	99.055
2	16	28	— 9.931	—14.724	98.625	216.796	146.224
3	36	61	10.069	18.276	101.385	334.012	184.021
4	31	39	5.069	— 3.724	25.695	13.868	— 18.877
5	27	38	1.069	— 4.724	1.143	22.316	— 5.050
6	29	51	3.069	8.276	9.419	68.492	25.399
7	36	59	10.069	16.276	101.385	264.908	163.883
8	38	61	12.069	18.276	145.661	334.012	220.573
9	33	61	7.069	18.276	49.971	334.012	129.193
10	20	39	— 5.931	— 3.724	35.177	13.868	22.087
11	11	34	—14.931	— 8.724	222.935	76.108	130.258
12	15	32	—10.931	—10.724	119.487	115.004	117.224
13	28	38	2.069	— 4.724	4.281	22.316	— 9.774
14	38	55	12.069	12.276	145.661	150.700	148.159
15	25	46	— 0.931	3.276	0.867	10.732	— 3.050
16	25	43	— 0.931	0.276	0.867	0.076	— 0.257
17	20	22	— 5.931	—20.724	35.177	429.484	122.914
18	14	25	—11.931	—17.724	142.349	314.140	211.465
19	19	35	— 6.931	—· 7.724	48.039	59.660	53.535
20	35	54	9.069	11.276	82.247	127.148	102.262
21	32	43	6.069	0.276	36.833	0.076	1.675
22	32	49	6.069	6.276	36.833	39.388	38.089
23	18	25	— 7.931	—17.724	62.901	314.140	140.569
24	13	19	—12.931	—23.724	167.211	562.828	306.775
25	27	40	1.069	— 2.724	1.143	7.420	— 2.912
26	17	43	— 8.931	0.276	79.763	0.076	— 2.465
27	32	45	6.069	2.276	36.833	5.180	13.813
28	28	53	2.069	10.276	4.281	105.596	21.261
29	23	46	— 2.931	3.276	8.591	10.732	— 9.602
T = 752		1239				1869.869	4103.788	2346.447
M = 25.931		42.724				64.478	141.510	

$$r = \frac{\Sigma xy}{N\sigma_x\sigma_y}$$

$$r = \frac{2346.447}{29\ (\ \sqrt{64.478 \times 141.510}\ )}$$

$$r = \frac{2346.447}{29\ (\ \sqrt{9124.282}\ )}$$

$$r = \frac{2346.447}{29 \times 95.521}$$

$$r = \frac{2346.447}{2770.109}$$

$$r = .847$$

Steps for calculating the product-moment r by the raw score method using the formula

$$r = \frac{\frac{\Sigma XY}{N} - M_X M_Y}{SD_X SD_Y}$$

as illustrated in Table XXIII follow:

1. List the names or numbers of the students whose pairs of scores are involved in column 1.

2. Indicate the pairs of scores (X and Y) for each student in columns 2 and 3.

3. Show the squares of the X scores and Y scores in columns 4 and 5.

4. In column 6 indicate the product of each student's scores on the X and Y tests.

5. Add the values in columns 2, 3, 4, 5, and 6 to obtain the ΣX (752), ΣY (1239), ΣX^2 (21370), ΣY^2 (57039) and ΣXY (34475) respectively. The numerical values pertain to the data in Table XXIII. Divide the ΣX

TABLE XXIII

CALCULATION OF THE PRODUCT-MOMENT r USING THE
RAW SCORE METHOD

1	2	3	4	5	6
Subj.	X	Y	X^2	Y^2	XY
1.	34	55	1156	3025	1870
2.	16	28	256	784	448
3.	36	61	1296	3721	2196
4.	31	39	961	1521	1209
5.	27	38	729	1444	1026
6.	29	51	841	2601	1479
7.	36	59	1296	3481	2124
8.	38	61	1444	3721	2318
9.	33	61	1089	3721	2013
10.	20	39	400	1521	780
11.	11	34	121	1156	374
12.	15	32	225	1024	480
13.	28	38	784	1444	1064
14.	38	55	1444	3025	2090
15.	25	46	625	2116	1150
16.	25	43	625	1849	1075
17.	20	22	400	484	440
18.	14	25	196	625	350
19.	19	35	361	1225	665
20.	35	54	1225	2916	1890
21.	32	43	1024	1849	1376
22.	32	49	1024	2401	1568
23.	18	25	324	625	450
24.	13	19	169	361	247
25.	27	40	729	1600	1080
26.	17	43	289	1849	731
27.	32	45	1024	2025	1440
28.	28	53	784	2809	1484
29.	23	46	529	2116	1058
T =	752	1239	21370	57039	34475
M =	25.931	42.724	736.897	1966.862	1188.793
M^2 =	672.417	1825.340			

$$r = \frac{\frac{\Sigma XY}{N} - M_X M_Y}{SD_X SD_Y}$$

$$SD_X = \sqrt{\frac{\Sigma X^2}{N} - M_X^2}$$

$$SD_X = \sqrt{\frac{21370}{29} - 25.931^2}$$

$$SD_X = \sqrt{736.897 - 672.417}$$

$$SD_X = \sqrt{64.480}$$

$$SD_X = 8.030$$

$$SD_Y = \sqrt{\frac{\Sigma Y^2}{N} - M_Y^2}$$

$$SD_Y = \sqrt{\frac{57039}{29} - 42.724^2}$$

$$SD_Y = \sqrt{1966.862 - 1825.340}$$

$$SD_Y = \sqrt{141.522}$$

$$SD_Y = 11.896$$

$$r = \frac{\frac{34475}{29} - (25.931 \times 42.724)}{8.030 \times 11.896}$$

$$r = \frac{1188.793 - 1107.876}{95.525}$$

$$r = \frac{80.917}{95.525} \qquad r = .847$$

and the ΣY by N (29) to obtain the means of the score values in columns 2 and 3 which are 25.931 and 42.724 respectively.

$$\text{The mean of the } \Sigma XY \text{ is } \frac{\Sigma XY}{N} \text{ or } 1188.793$$

6. Square the means for the scores on X (672.417) and Y (1825.340).

7. Compute the standard deviations for the X and Y scores. The method is outlined in Chapter 6 when standard deviation is calculated by the Raw Score Method using the formula

$$SD = \sqrt{\frac{\Sigma X^2}{N} - M^2}$$

Make the substitutions in the formula for SD_X and SD_Y as illustrated by the data above in Table XXIII.

8. Make the substitutions in the formula for r which consists of dividing the ΣXY by N from which the product of M_X and M_Y is subtracted. The remainder is divided by the the product of SD_X and SD_Y. The result is the product moment coefficient which for our illustration is .847.

Computation of the Pearsonian r from a double-entry table as illustrated in Table XXIV follows:

TABLE XXIV

CORRELATION COEFFICIENT BETWEEN THE SCORES OBTAINED ON THE H AND SA READING TESTS

Class Interval	10-11	12-13	14-15	16-17	18-19	20-21	22-23	24-25	26-27	28-29	30-31	32-33	34-35	36-37	38-39	f_y	d_y	fd_y	fd_y^2	xy
60-62										/			/	/		3	8	24	192	160
57-59												/				1	7	7	49	49
54-56											//		/			3	6	18	108	120
51-53					//											2	5	10	50	30
48-50									/							1	4	4	16	20
45-47				/ /							/					3	3	9	27	18
42-44			/			/					/					3	2	6	12	6
39-41				/				/	/							3	1	3	3	5
36-38								/	/							2	0	0	0	0
33-35	/			/												2	-1	-2	2	8
30-32		/														1	-2	-2	4	8
27-29			/													1	-3	-3	9	9
24-26			/	/												2	-4	-8	32	24
21-23					/											1	-5	-5	25	5
18-20		/														1	-6	-6	36	30
f_x	1	1	2	2	2	2	1	2	2	3	1	4	2	2	2	29		55	565	492
d_x	-6	-5	-4	-3	-2	-1	0	1	2	3	4	5	6	7	8					
fd_x	-6	-5	-8	-6	-4	-2	0	2	4	9	4	20	12	14	16	50				
fd_x^2	36	25	32	18	8	2	0	2	8	27	16	100	72	98	128	572				

X (H Reading Test) — Y (SA Reading Tests)

1. Prepare a double-entry table as illustrated in Table XXIV.

2. Set up a frequency distribution across the top (X-axis) for the Test H Reading scores in the same manner as was done in Chapter 3, with the smallest interval to the extreme left.

3. Set up a frequency distribution on the left side of the double-entry table (Y-axis) for the SA Reading scores. The two frequency distributions need not have the same number of intervals nor the same size intervals.

4. Enter the pairs of scores for each student. One tally mark for each student will show the size of the score obtained on two tests. Student number 1, Table XXI, obtained an H Reading Test score of 34 and a SA Reading Test score of 55. The cell that contains the tally for the scores obtained on the two tests is the fifth cell downward (counting used and unused cells) under the interval 34-35, which is directly to the right of interval 54-56. Student number 2 obtained an H Reading Test score of 16 and a SA Reading Test score of 28. The cell that contains the tally for the scores obtained on the two tests is the 14th cell down from the interval 16-17 and directly to the right of interval 27-29. All scores are tabulated in the same manner.

Calculations for Table 24

X-Axis	Y-Axis

$$c_x = \frac{\Sigma fd_x}{N} = \frac{50}{29} = 1.724 \qquad\qquad c_y = \frac{\Sigma fd_y}{N} = \frac{55}{29} = 1.897$$

$$c_x^2 = 1.724^2 = 2.972 \qquad\qquad c_y^2 = 1.897^2 = 3.599$$

$$\frac{\Sigma fd_x^2}{N} = \frac{572}{29} = 19.724 \qquad\qquad \frac{\Sigma fd_y^2}{N} = \frac{565}{29} = 19.483$$

$$\sigma_x = \sqrt{\frac{\Sigma fd_x^2}{N} - c_x^2} \qquad\qquad \sigma_y = \sqrt{\frac{\Sigma fd_x^2}{N} - c_y^2}$$

$$\sigma_x = \sqrt{19.724 - 2.972} \qquad\qquad \sigma_y = \sqrt{19.483 - 3.599}$$

$$\sigma_x = \sqrt{16.752} \qquad\qquad \sigma_y = \sqrt{15.884}$$

$$\sigma_x = 4.093 \ (\text{In Steps}) \qquad\qquad \sigma_y = 3.985 \ (\text{In Steps})$$

$$c_x c_y = 1.724 \times 1.897 = 3.270$$

$$\sigma_x \sigma_y = 4.093 \times 3.985 = 16.311$$

$$r = \frac{\dfrac{\Sigma xy}{N} - c_x c_y}{\sigma_x \sigma_y} = \frac{16.966 - 3.270}{4.093 \times 3.985} = \frac{13.696}{16.311} = .840$$

5. Add the tabulations in each column under the X-axis and place the sum in the f_x cell. Add the tallies in each row for the Y-axis and place the sum in the f_y cell at the end of each row. Summate the frequencies for the Y data and X data. The total should be the same, which is 29 in Table XXIV.

6. Complete the columns f_y, d_y, fd_y and fd_y^2. Complete the f_x, d_x, fd_x and fd_x^2 rows. Enter the totals for the rows and columns as indicated in Table XXIV. The steps in calculating this phase of the Pearson product-moment r are the same as the steps used when calculating the standard deviation described in Chapter 6, except that the standard deviation values are not multiplied by the size of the class interval. The correlation coefficient is calculated on the basis of class interval units and not on the basis of scale distance.

7. As shown by the calculations performed to obtain the product-moment correlation when using a double-entry table $c_x = 1.724$, $c_x^2 = 2.972$, $c_y = 1.897$ and $c_y^2 = 3.599$.

8. Substitute the appropriate values in the formula for σ_x and σ_y. The standard deviation in steps for the x scores is 4.093 and for the y scores it is 3.985. Sigma x times sigma y $= 16.311$ and c_x times $c_y = 3.270$.

9. The xy values on the double-entry table are determined as follows: Use one row at a time. Multiply the cases in each cell by their "d" shown below and the "d" at the right end of the row. Find the algebraic sum of these products for the entire row or class interval and place it in the xy cell at the end of the row. To illustrate further, we will use the row represented by the interval 42-44. There is one tally under the interval 16-17 (X-axis) with a deviation of —3 and a deviation of 2 on the Y-axis which results in $1 \times -3 \times 2 = -6$. There is one tally under the interval 24-25 (X-axis) with a deviation of 1 and a deviation of 2 on the Y-axis which results in $1 \times 1 \times 2 = 2$. Likewise there is one tally under the interval 32-33 (X-axis) with a deviation of 5 and a deviation of 2 on the Y-axis which results in $1 \times 5 \times 2 = 10$. This includes all the tallies in the row represented by the interval 42-44 and the algebraic sum of the three values is $-6 + 2 + 10 = 6$ which is the xy value for the row represented by the interval 42-44. The xy column must be similarly completed for each row of tallies with the total (492) entered in the appropriate space.

$$\frac{\Sigma xy}{N} = \frac{492}{29} = 16.966$$

10. Substitute in the formula

$$r = \frac{\dfrac{\Sigma xy}{N} - c_x c_y}{\sigma_x \sigma_y}$$

to solve for r.

$$r = \frac{\dfrac{492}{29} - 3.270}{16.311} = \frac{16.966 - 3.270}{16.311} = \frac{13.696}{16.311} = .840.$$

The correlation coefficient is very close to the r obtained in our previous illustrations. The slight difference may be attributed to the grouping error in the frequency distributions of the double-entry table.

The data shown in Table XXV are concerned with the same 29 students who took the H Reading Test (X-axis) and the SA Reading Test (Y-axis). However, 10 was subtracted from each H Reading Test score and 18 was subtracted from each SA Reading Test score. The frequency distributions in the double-entry table for the H Test and the SA Test must be revised accordingly. When the double-entry table procedure is used, all the numerical values, other than the size of the intervals which have been reduced by subtracting a constant value from each one, are the same. As can be readily observed by referring to Table XXV, there is not the saving of time and labor with the size of the scores reduced when using a double-entry table that there is when other methods of procedure for obtaining a correlation coefficient are used.

When calculating coefficients of correlation for given distributions, it is not the size of the scores that represent the important consideration. Rather it is the discrepancy between the larger numbers over the smaller numbers in each distribution that is significant. A constant may be subtracted from each score value for each distribution. This suggestion was first introduced by L. P. Ayres.[18] A number that is one less than the smallest number in each distribution may be subtracted. This procedure systematically reduces the size of the numerical values that one must use in performing the calculations. When the calculations are performed without mechanical aids there is a considerable saving in time and labor when procedures other than the double-entry table are used.

18. Ayres, L. P.: "Substituting Small Numbers for Large Ones in the Computation of Coefficient Correlations," *Journal of Educational Research*, 2:502-504, June, 1920.

TABLE XXV

SCATTER DIAGRAM REPRESENTING DATA USED IN TABLE XXIV
WITH A CONSTANT SUBTRACTED FROM EACH SCORE
FOR EACH VARIABLE

		X (H Reading Test)																f_y	d_y	fd_y	fd_y^2	xy
	Class Interval	0-1	2-3	4-5	6-7	8-9	10-11	12-13	14-15	16-17	18-19	20-21	22-23	24-25	26-27	28-29						
	42-44										/			/		/			3	8	24	192	160
	39-41												/						1	7	7	49	49
Y	36-38												//		/				3	6	18	108	120
S A	33-35								//										2	5	10	50	30
	30-32											/							1	4	4	16	20
R e	27-29				/	/						/							3	3	9	27	18
a d	24-26			/				/				/							3	2	6	12	6
i n	21-23				/				/		/								3	1	3	3	5
g	18-20							/	/										2	0	0	0	0
T e	15-17	/			/														2	-1	-2	2	8
s t	12-14			/															1	-2	-2	4	8
	9-11				/														1	-3	-3	9	9
	6-8			/	/														2	-4	-8	32	24
	3-5					/													1	-5	-5	25	5
	0-2		/																1	-6	-6	36	30
	f_x	1	1	2	2	2	2	1	2	2	3	1	4	2	2	2			29		55	565	492
	d_x	-6	-5	-4	-3	-2	-1	0	1	2	3	4	5	6	7	8							
	fd_x	-6	-5	-8	-6	-4	-2	0	2	4	9	4	20	12	14	16			50				
	fd_x^2	36	25	32	18	8	2	0	2	8	27	16	100	72	98	128			572				

RANK DIFFERENCE METHOD FOR COMPUTING THE COEFFICIENT OF CORRELATION

The rank-difference method (rho) of obtaining a coefficient of correlation as proposed by C. E. Spearman is a comparatively simple procedure. Each score in the two series of scores is assigned a rank. The largest score is assigned a rank of 1; the next largest, a rank of 2; etc. The scores in Table XXVI are the same scores used in the previous tables pertaining to the calculation of a coefficient of correlation. Column 4 shows the rank of the X scores. The largest X score is 38. Since there are two scores of 38 we cannot assign one a rank of 1 and the other a rank of 2 but we must average the ranks of 1 and 2

$$\frac{1+2}{2} = 1.5$$

and assign the rank of 1.5 to both scores. The next score in size is 36 and there are two scores of 36 so we average the ranks of 3 and 4

$$\frac{3+4}{2} = 3.5$$

and assign the rank of 3.5 to each of the two scores. The next lower score is 35 and it is assigned a rank of 5.0.

To illustrate tied scores further we will enter column 5 rank of Y scores. The largest score is 61 of which there are three so we average ranks 1, 2, and 3

$$\frac{1+2+3}{3} = 2$$

and assign the rank of 2 to each of the three scores. The next lower score is 59 and it is assigned the rank of 4, and so forth.

Steps in calculation of rho are the following:

1. List the students or numbers and the two scores obtained, (columns 1, 2, and 3).

2. Assign a rank order to each score within each series, (columns 4 and 5).

3. Show the difference (D) in rank between each student's scores (column 6). It is not necessary to show negative values but it may help to facilitate accuracy.

4. Square the differences in ranks which is represented by D^2, (column 7). The sum of the D^2 column is 566.0.

5. Make the necessary substitutions in the formula

$$\text{rho} = 1 - \frac{6\Sigma D^2}{N(N^2 - 1)}$$

The calculations are shown in connection with Table XXVI. The rho obtained (.861) compares fairly closely with the correlation obtained in the preceding illustrations.

The Spearman Foot-Rule, $R = 1 - \dfrac{6\Sigma G}{N^2 - 1}$

The Foot-Rule is illustrated in Table XXVII. The G in the Spearman Foot-Rule or short method has reference to the gain in rank of the second series of ranks over the first series of ranks. This is indicated by column 6 in Table XXVII. Student number 1 for example has scores that rank 6.0 on Test X and 5.5 on Test Y which represents a gain of 0.5 (his rank is 0.5 higher or better on the second series of scores). Student number 2 has scores with identical ranks, hence the gain is 0.0. Student number 4 has scores with ranks of 11.0 and 18.5 respectively. His score in the second series is lower than it is in the first series, hence his gain is designated as zero (0.0).

The calculations and substitutions are shown in connection with the data shown in Table XXVII. When a comparison is made between the results obtained when using the Spearman Rank-Difference method and the Spearman Foot-Rule Method (Tables XXVI and XXVII), it becomes obvious why the Foot-Rule is seldom used.

TABLE XXVI

RANK-DIFFERENCE CORRELATION

1 Subj.	2 Sc X	3 Sc Y	4 R_X	5 R_Y	6 D	7 D^2
1	34	55	6.0	5.5	0.5	0.25
2	16	28	25.0	25.0	0.0	0.0
3	36	61	3.5	2.0	1.5	2.25
4	31	39	11.0	18.5	7.5	56.25
5	27	38	15.5	20.5	5.0	25.0
6	29	51	12.0	9.0	3.0	9.0
7	36	59	3.5	4.0	0.5	0.25
8	38	61	1.5	2.0	0.5	0.25
9	33	61	7.0	2.0	5.0	25.0
10	20	39	20.5	18.5	2.0	4.0
11	11	34	29.0	23.0	6.0	36.0
12	15	32	26.0	24.0	2.0	4.0
13	28	38	13.5	20.5	7.0	49.0
14	38	55	1.5	5.5	4.0	16.0
15	25	46	17.5	11.5	6.0	36.0
16	25	43	17.5	15.0	2.5	6.25
17	20	22	20.5	28.0	7.5	56.25
18	14	25	27.0	26.5	0.5	0.25
19	19	35	22.0	22.0	0.0	0.0
20	35	54	5.0	7.0	2.0	4.0
21	32	43	9.0	15.0	6.0	36.0
22	32	49	9.0	10.0	1.0	1.0
23	18	25	23.0	26.5	3.5	12.25
24	13	19	28.0	29.0	1.0	1.0
25	27	40	15.5	17.0	1.5	2.25
26	17	43	24.0	15.0	9.0	81.0
27	32	45	9.0	13.0	4.0	16.0
28	28	53	13.5	8.0	5.5	30.25
29	23	46	19.0	11.5	7.5	56.25
N = 29						566.0

Calculations

$$\text{Rho} = 1 - \frac{6\Sigma D^2}{N(N^2 - 1)} \qquad \text{Rho} = 1 - \frac{3396}{24360}$$

$$\text{Rho} = 1 - \frac{6 \times 566.000}{29(841 - 1)} \qquad \text{Rho} = 1 - .139$$

$$\text{Rho} = 1 - \frac{6 \times 566.000}{29 \times 840} \qquad \text{Rho} = .861$$

TABLE XXVII

APPLICATION OF SPEARMAN FOOT-RULE

1 Subj.	2 Sc X	3 Sc Y	4 R_X	5 R_Y	6 G
1	34	55	6.0	5.5	0.5
2	16	28	25.0	25.0	0.0
3	36	61	3.5	2.0	1.5
4	31	39	11.0	18.5	0.0
5	27	38	15.5	20.5	0.0
6	29	51	12.0	9.0	3.0
7	36	59	3.5	4.0	0.0
8	38	61	1.5	2.0	0.0
9	33	61	7.0	2.0	5.0
10	20	39	20.5	18.5	2.0
11	11	34	29.0	23.0	6.0
12	15	32	26.0	24.0	2.0
13	28	38	13.5	20.5	0.0
14	38	55	1.5	5.5	0.0
15	25	46	17.5	11.5	6.0
16	25	43	17.5	15.0	2.5
17	20	22	20.5	28.0	0.0
18	14	25	27.0	26.5	0.5
19	19	35	22.0	22.0	0.0
20	35	54	5.0	7.0	0.0
21	32	43	9.0	15.0	0.0
22	32	49	9.0	10.0	0.0
23	18	25	23.0	26.5	0.0
24	13	19	28.0	29.0	0.0
25	27	40	15.5	17.0	0.0
26	17	43	24.0	15.0	9.0
27	32	45	9.0	13.0	0.0
28	28	53	13.5	8.0	5.5
29	23	46	19.0	11.5	7.5

N = 29   51.0

Calculations

$$R = 1 - \frac{6\Sigma G}{N^2 - 1} \qquad R = 1 - \frac{306}{840}$$

$$\qquad\qquad\qquad\qquad R = 1 - .364$$

$$R = 1 - \frac{6 \times 51}{841 - 1} \qquad R = .636$$

INTERPRETATION OF CORRELATIONS

When the procedures for calculating a correlation coefficient have been mastered, the question how the coefficient of correlation should be interpreted still remains. The significance of the size of the correlation, whether positive or negative, depends upon a number of factors that make it almost impossible to categorize situations and size of coefficients.

For the purpose of this discussion, "significant" should be interpreted to mean that the correlation is significantly different from zero or that it is due to something other than chance.

When a low correlation, one that approaches zero—positive or negative, is obtained for two variables in a sample, we may feel that there is a relationship. However, the two variables may not be correlated in the specified universe or total population from which the samples were drawn. The low correlation could easily have occurred by chance or accident. The basic assumption then is that the obtained r does not differ significantly from zero until demonstrated otherwise.

SMALL SAMPLE CORRELATION COEFFICIENT

When a sample or number of pairs (N) is small, which could be considered in the range of 12 to 25 or 30 pairs, a t-test for determining the significance of r can be used. The formula frequently employed is

$$t = r \sqrt{\frac{N - 2}{1 - r^2}}.^*$$

The r value substituted in the formula is the correlation coefficient that is obtained and the N value represents the number of pairs of observations used in calculating the r. Reference should be made to a table containing data that show coefficients of correlation and t-ratios significant at the 1 percent (.01) and 5 percent (.05) levels of confidence, or it may be said that we may be highly confident or reasonably confident that the obtained r differs significantly from zero, providing the obtained t-ratio is sufficiently large. Most authors of statistics textbooks provide such tables in the appendices.

The application of the formula

$$t = r \sqrt{\frac{N - 2}{1 - r^2}}$$

in connection with the correlation coefficient .85 and the N of 29

*Fisher

used in Tables XXI to XXIII is illustrated by making the appropriate substitutions as follows:

Illustration 5

$$t = .85 \sqrt{\frac{29 - 2}{1 - r^2}} \qquad t = .85 \sqrt{96.43}$$

$$t = .85 \sqrt{\frac{27}{1 - .72}} \qquad t = .85 \times 9.82$$

$$t = .85 \sqrt{\frac{27}{.28}} \qquad t = 8.35$$

By referring to Ferguson[19] who provides a convenient table (based on Fisher and Yates) of critical values of correlation coefficients, we may determine whether or not our obtained r of .85 for the 29 pairs of observations is significantly different from zero. Since our $N = 29$, we enter the raw degrees of freedom (df) 27, ($N - 2$) under the .01 (or 1 percent level) column. The required t-ratio or critical value of 2.771 is exceeded in our illustration where the t value is 8.35. Therefore, we may reject the null hypothesis and be highly confident or be confident beyond the 1 percent level (.01) that our obtained correlation of .85 differs significantly from zero. Had our t-ratio been less than .471 but .367 or more, we would have accepted the 5 percent level of confidence and we could be reasonably confident that our obtained r was not due to chance. As is shown in Table B (Ferguson), there are occasions when other levels of confidence may be used.

The techniques outlined above have been kept simple but they should be of some help. However, the discussion represents only a meager introduction to the mathematically complicated area of the correlation coefficient concept.

PREDICTING AN UNKNOWN SCORE IN ONE VARIABLE FROM A KNOWN SCORE IN THE OTHER VARIABLE

The accuracy of the predictions made depends largely on the size of the correlation obtained between the two variables under consideration. Zero correlations are useless for purposes of prediction

19. Ferguson, George A.: *Statistical Analysis in Psychology and Education*, 2nd ed. New York, McGraw-Hill, 1966, p. 406, Table B. (Also see any statistics book with a table of critical values of r.)

and small correlation coefficients have large errors of estimate or prediction. The larger the correlation, the more accurate are the predictions that can be made. The standard error of estimate shows the amount by which a score obtained on a test may differ from a hypothetically "true" score.

To predict an H Reading (x column or X-axis on scatter diagram) Test score from what we know about the SA Reading Test (y column or Y-axis on scatter diagram) requires the use of the score form of the regression equation which is

$$X' = r_{xy} \frac{\sigma_x}{\sigma_y} (Y - M_y) + M_x$$

On the other hand, if we were to predict an SA Reading Test score, the regression equation would be

$$Y' = r_{xy} \frac{\sigma_y}{\sigma_x} (X - M_x) + M_y$$

Let us assume that we know that an examinee obtained a score of 34 on the H Reading Test but that he does not have a score on the SA Reading Test. We, however, wish to predict his score (Y') on the SA Reading Test. The data in Table XXIII provide all the numerical values required to make the necessary substitutions in the formula above which is

$$Y' = r_{xy} \frac{\sigma_y}{\sigma_x} (X - M_x) + M_y$$

Illustration 6

$$Y' = .85 \times \frac{11.90}{8.03} (34 - 25.93) + 42.72$$
$$Y' = .85 \times 1.48 \times 8.07 + 42.72$$
$$Y' = 1.26 \times 8.07 + 42.72$$
$$Y' = 10.17 + 42.72$$
$$Y' = 52.89 \text{ or } 53$$

Consequently we would predict that if the student's H Test score is 34 his SA Reading Test score would be approximately 53.

The reverse of the situation would be that we know a student's SA Reading Test score which for the illustration is 55 but that we do not have a H Reading Test score for him. To predict the most likely score that he might have obtained on the H Reading Test we would make the necessary substitutions in the formula

$$X' = r_{xy} \frac{\sigma_x}{\sigma_y} (Y - M_y) + M_x$$

We would again refer to the data in Table XXIII.

Illustration 7

$$X' = .85 \times \frac{8.03}{11.90}(55 - 42.72) + 25.93$$
$$X' = .85 \times .67 \times 12.28 + 25.93$$
$$X' = .57 \times 12.28 + 25.93$$
$$X' = 7.00 + 25.93$$
$$X' = 32.93 \text{ or } 33$$

Hence, we would predict that the student who obtained a score of 55 on the SA Reading Test would obtain a score somewhere around 33 on the H Reading Test.

The data in Table XXIII were used in the two illustrations to predict Y from our information about X and to predict X from our information about Y. Had we used the data in Table XXIV which is a double-entry table it would have been necessary to do additional calculations.

In the double-entry table we solved for sigma in steps so it would have been necessary to multiply the X and Y sigma values by the size of the respective class intervals from which they were derived. Also it would have been necessary to calculate the mean for the scores representing the X and Y axes.

STANDARD ERROR OF ESTIMATE

When predictions are made on the basis of regression equations, as we did above, it is possible to find the standard error of estimate from the coefficient of correlation obtained between the two variables.

To find the standard error of estimate for the predicted Y' score (53) (SA Reading Test), we would use the formula

$$\sigma_{xy} = \sigma_y \sqrt{1 - r_{xy}^2}$$

Substitution of the appropriate numerical values in the formula will provide us with the standard error of estimate. The numerical values to be substituted may be obtained from either of the two preceding illustrations, 6 or 7.

We have predicted Y from X and made the observation that the variability of scores about the predicted score (Y') 53 obtained in Illustration 8 and the standard error of estimate is 6.31. We can be reasonably confident that if the person's X score is 34, then his Y score would lie somewhere between 53 ± 6.3 or 47.3 to 59.3.

Illustration 8

$$\sigma_{yx} = \sigma_y \sqrt{1 - r_{xy}^2}$$
$$\sigma_{yx} = 11.90 \sqrt{1 - .85^2}$$
$$\sigma_{yx} = 11.90 \sqrt{1 - .72}$$
$$\sigma_{yx} = 11.90 \sqrt{.28}$$
$$\sigma_{yx} = 11.90 \times .53$$
$$\sigma_{yx} = 6.31$$

When we predict X from Y we would change the standard error of estimate formula to read

$$\sigma_{xy} = \sigma_x \sqrt{1 - r_{xy}^2}$$

The values to be substituted in the formula can be obtained from Illustrations 6 or 7.

Illustration 9

$$\sigma_{xy} = \sigma_x \sqrt{1 - r_{xy}^2}$$
$$\sigma_{xy} = 8.03 \sqrt{1 - .85^2}$$
$$\sigma_{xy} = 8.03 \sqrt{1 - .72}$$
$$\sigma_{xy} = 8.03 \sqrt{.28}$$
$$\sigma_{xy} = 8.03 \times .53$$
$$\sigma_{xy} = 4.26$$

The predicted X score obtained is 33 and it should be associated with the standard error of estimate of 4.26. We can be reasonably confident that if the student's Y score is 53 that his X score will lie somewhere between 33 ± 4.3 or 28.7 to 37.3. (See Illus. 6 and 7.)

COEFFICIENT OF ALIENATION

The accuracy of predictions depends upon the size of the correlation coefficients. A simple formula

$$k = \sqrt{1 - r^2}$$

is used to calculate the coefficient of alienation. The k values in terms of percentages must then be subtracted from 100, which will provide us with the percentages of forecasting efficiency. Table XXVIII provides data obtained by the coefficient of alienation technique which show the percent of accuracy of predictions for a number of r values. The rapid increase in the loss of prediction efficiency as the correlation coefficient decreases in size should be noted.

TABLE XXVIII

PERCENT OF ACCURACY OF PREDICTIONS FOR EIGHTEEN r VALUES

r	% of Accuracy of Prediction	r	% of Accuracy of Prediction
1.00	100	.75	34
.99	86	.70	29
.98	80	.65	24
.97	76	.60	20
.96	72	.55	16
.93	63	.50	13
.90	56	.40	8
.85	47	.30	5
.80	40	.20	2

GENERAL REFERENCES

Greene, Harry A. *et al.*: *Measurement and Evaluation in the Elementary School,* 2nd ed. New York, Longmans, Green and Co., 1953, pp. 372-382.

Johnson, Palmer O. and Robert W. B. Jackson: *Introduction to Statistical Methods*. New York, Prentice-Hall, 1953, pp. 271, 275-286.

Noll, Victor H.: *Introduction to Educational Measurement*. Boston, Houghton Mifflin, 1957, pp. 45-51, 407-411.

Remmers, H. H. and N. L. Gage: *Educational Measurement and Evaluation,* Rev. ed. New York, Harper and Brothers, 1955, pp. 593-600.

Thorndike, Robert L. and Elizabeth Hagen: *Measurement and Evaluation in Psychology and Education,* 2nd ed. New York, John Wiley and Sons, 1961, pp. 567-570, 116-122.

10 DESIRABLE CHARACTERISTICS OF MEASURING INSTRUMENTS

T<small>HE</small> qualities inherent in a good measuring instrument cannot be overestimated when setting up a basic evaluation program. Of equal importance are the characteristics of instruments and techniques that should supplement any phase of the basic guidance and counseling program. The authors of tests and technical manuals usually provide a variety of statistical data that are helpful in selecting measuring instruments. The general format should also be considered as well as the content of achievement and certain scholastic aptitude tests.

Several specific and important characteristics of tests have been recognized for at least 50 years. For example, Otis[20] demonstrated the significance of test reliability in 1916. Other characteristics of tests were set forth by a committee on the psychological information of recruits in May, 1917. The work of Otis influenced the committee through L. M. Terman who was chairman of the committee. The Otis Score Card for Rating Tests[21] outlined criteria for rating tests, and in 1924 Ruch[22] devoted a chapter to the criteria of examinations. Spearman worked specifically with factor analysis early in the century (1901) as it pertained to test construction. Except for multiple factor analysis most of the work on desirable criteria or characteristics of tests has consisted of a further analysis and refinement of previously recognized characteristics.

20. Otis, Arthur S.: "Test Reliability of Spelling Scales Involving a 'Deviation Formula' for Correlation," *School and Society*, 4:716-722, November 11, 1916.

21. Otis, A. S.: "Scale for Rating Tests," *Test Service Bulletin* 13, New York, Harcourt, Brace and World.

22. Ruch, G. M.: *The Improvement of the Written Examination*, New York, Scott, Foresman and Company, 1924.

For persons with a comparatively high level of training there is an excellent monograph[23] that will serve as a guide to users as well as authors and producers of tests. There is no substitute for the appropriate use of tests.

VALIDITY

Without the characteristic of validity, a test is of no value for diagnostic, analytical or observational purposes. A diagnostic test points out specific weaknesses and strengths while an analytical test points out broader areas of strengths and weaknesses. We make observations by using testing instruments to make predictions more accurate, hence the importance of validity. The concept of validity is concerned with how well a test, psychological or educational, measures what it purports to measure. To be valid, a test must possess a high degree of reliability. Theoretically the validity coefficient cannot be higher than the square root of the reliability coefficient. The test score obtained must represent a relationship to some observable degree or measure of success. The evidence most frequently presented is a coefficient of correlation and it is stated as a *validity coefficient.*

Tests may be considered valid only when used in situations for which they were designed. A reading test may be valid for a relatively limited range level of ability. Likewise, a scholastic aptitude test is valid only for the level at which it was standardized. There may be exceptions at either end of the ability ranges. In such instances a higher level or lower level test as the case may be should be used.

Validity is a comparatively specific concept. It should not be thought of as something abstract. The examiner must be fully aware of the adequacy of the validity of a test in a given situation.

The descriptions of the several characteristics that follow are of importance not only when selecting standardized psychological and educational tests but also when informal (or teacher-made) tests are constructed.

Validity may be classified into two broad categories, one of which is characterized by reason (based on procedures or observations used to determine validity) while the other is based on sta-

23. *Standards for Educational and Psychological Tests and Manuals.* Washington, D. C., American Psychological Association, Inc., 1966.

tistical procedures, sometimes called empirical validity, which involves numerical values and statistical applications.

Face Validity

Face validity is on occasion confused with content validity. Technically it is not a kind of validity, but it may affect the overall validity of a test. The term face validity pertains more specifically to the appropriateness of the vocabulary and content used in the construction of the test and the appropriateness of the concepts that are sampled. For example, if the test is designed for aviation metalsmiths the vocabulary and concepts tested should, insofar as practical, be based on vocabulary, content and settings pertaining to the field for which the test is administered. Briefly stated, the examinee should not consider the content of the test absurd. However, a few examinees may consider some questions foolish even in the best of tests. The factor of face validity may be negligible in some tests and of considerable importance in others as it may affect objective validity as well as the attitude of the examinee toward the test.

Content Validity

Content validity is especially important in achievement or educational tests and special branches of knowledge or skills. The test items should represent an adequate sample of a well defined area of content. Each item should sample what the total instrument is designed to measure.

Concurrent Validity

Concurrent validity is also known as status validity. In this type of validity a given test is compared with an approved contemporary criterion. The results of the two tests may be obtained in the same day or within a relatively few days. An example may be the comparison of the results obtained on a scholastic aptitude test and an achievement test.

Congruent Validity

Congruent validity pertains to the comparison of results of two tests of the same type. In other words, the results obtained on a group test of scholastic aptitude may be compared with the results obtained on other group tests of ability, or the results obtained may be compared with the results obtained on individual tests of mental ability.

A new test need not correlate perfectly with an established test, for if it did there may not be a need for the "new" test. However, if in this instance one test is a group test and the other test is an individual test, it could be a highly desirable situation. If one group test requires significantly less time to administer than the group test with which it is compared, then there again could be a decided advantage. When the correlation between two tests is not high, the question still remains as to which one of the two tests is the better or are the two tests different.

Predictive Validity

Predictive validity in some respects resembles concurrent validity, except that the criterion measure with which the new test is compared is based on scores obtained at a later time. For example, a period of instruction, or training in specific skills may occur between the time the new test is administered and the criterion measure results are obtained.

Construct Validity

Construct validity is usually used when an appropriate independent criterion is not accessible or available. The author of a test may have a well defined concept in mind upon which he wishes to base his test items but there may be no independent criterion available. This is especially true in the areas of interests, attitudes, understandings, or awareness of aesthetic values. The procedures, designs and techniques used when construct validity is relied upon are based upon the construct or concept the test constructor has in mind that he wishes to measure.

Discriminative Capacity as a Type of Validity

Discriminative capacity as a type of validity was recognized by Kuhlmann in 1928.[24] He had no quarrel with empirical means of establishing the validity of a test of mental ability, but he also believed that it could result in misleading results or erroneous conclusions. Discriminative capacity pertains to the examinee's ability to show

24. Kuhlmann, F.: "The Kuhlmann-Anderson Intelligence Tests Compared with Seven Others," *Journal of Applied Psychology*, December, 1928.

increments of growth in mental development.[25] Pintner[26] placed considerable confidence in establishing validity for mental ability tests by using the concept of discriminative capacity based on increase in scores from age group to age group, particularly when it did not involve specific training.

Factorial Validity

Factorial validity is concerned chiefly with differentiation of groups of abilities. Each subtest should yield a low correlation with the other subtests or factors that make up the total test. The basic point of departure consists of an analysis of intercorrelations (correlation matrix) among relatively limited areas or measures. There are several methods that can be used for categorizing a number of variables into common factors or clusters. The techniques of factor analysis are usually presented in advanced textbooks in statistics in psychology. It is not a purely mechanical procedure and it ends in what may be called a factor matrix.

The factors or clusters that result in scholastic aptitude tests are sometimes called "primary mental abilities." The aim is to construct tests that consist of a few subtests each of which is relatively independent of the others. The subtests may be sufficiently independent to be used as individual tests, or the scores on the subtests may be combined (perhaps profile-wise) to provide a composite score.

When factorial or differential validity is implied or claimed for a test, it may be informative to examine the appropriate manuals to observe the correlations among the subtests.

RELIABILITY

The concept of the reliability of a test pertains to the accuracy with which the test measures that which it does measure, or we could say how consistently does the test measure what it purports to measure. Variations in consistency of measurement may be affected by faulty test construction and individual differences among the persons to whom the test is administered. The consistency with which an instrument measures from one administration to another is in-

25. *Kuhlmann-Anderson Tests—Instruction Manual*, Minneapolis,, Minnesota, Educational Test Bureau, 1942. (Now revised and published by Personnell Press, Inc., Princeton, New Jersey, 1952.)

26. *Pintner General Ability Tests, Non-Language Series, Manual of Directions*, 1945, p. 5.

fluenced by the extent to which the obtained scores are free from faulty construction of items and improper standardization procedures. The reliability coefficient is basically intended to reflect inconsistency in individual performance and such chance factors as may operate.

A reliability coefficient of 70 to 75 is satisfactory for group analyses. For individual diagnoses, approximately 85 or higher is desirable.

It is well-known that psychological or educational tests are not one hundred percent accurate. Every score obtained is influenced by the inaccuracies of the instrument itself. However, the scores obtained on a valid test represent mainly the ability, knowledge and information the examinee possesses.

From the previous discussion it is evident that a test may be statistically reliable but not valid in a given situation. Also, a test cannot be valid unless it is reliable. The reliability data for tests are usually presented in technical manuals that are prepared to accompany the supplementary materials for a test. The reliability values are usually expressed by means of a single coefficient of correlation. Hence, the relationship of certain aspects of a test to its reliability.

It may be said that other things being equal, within reasonable limitations (such as length of test period), the longer the test the higher the reliability coefficient may be. This is also related to the range of scores obtainable on a test. It is conceivable that a test designed to measure a certain ability for grades three through ten may be affected in that manner. If there is only one reliability coefficient indicated for the test, it could easily be high and the test would measure most consistently at the sixth or seventh grade level. However, for the third or fourth grade level, only a relatively short portion of the test could be responded to by most of the examinees, and by the same token, only the upper end of the test would be functional for most of the ninth and tenth graders. In effect it would represent a relatively short test for either end of the grade range.

Typical Forms of Reliability

Commonly used methods of determining test reliability are based on the consistency of the scores obtained by the examinees in a given population when two distributions of scores for them are obtained and correlated. The Richardson-Kuder formula (20) is especially appropriate when one has one form of a test and the items are approximately equal in difficulty.

Coefficient of Equivalence

The coefficient of equivalence is obtained by the administration of two equivalent forms of the same test to the same population. The tests are designed so that the two forms of the test are quite uniform in the characteristics that make up the test. Calculating the correlation coefficient between the two sets of scores obtained from two equivalent forms is especially desirable when the tests are speed tests rather than power tests.

Coefficient of Stability

When the coefficient of stability is established, it is accomplished by administering one form of a test twice to the same population (test-retest). The coefficient of correlation between the two sets of scores is then calculated. It is important that not too much time elapse between administrations of the test. Approximately two weeks is a reasonable time. This allows somewhat for reduction in transfer of training, and, as the time that elapses between administration of the test increases, the obtained coefficient of correlation tends to drop.

The retest method does assure complete equivalence in test content. On the other hand retention of specific information would tend to reduce the significance of the coefficient of stability. This is a more influential factor with achievement tests than with mental ability tests. When the element of speed is emphasized in a test, the coefficient of stability tends to be a good indicator of the reliability of the test.

Coefficient of Internal Consistency

1. *Split-half or chance-half method.* The two terms usually are used interchangeably. In either case two half-scores are obtained for each examinee on the basis of halves of the test. The halves may consist of odd and even items (split-half) or the items may be picked at random and placed in each of two halves of the test (chance-half). When the items are arranged according to difficulty it is more appropriate and also convenient to use the scores on the odd items and the even items. The coefficient of correlation is calculated between the scores obtained on the odd and even items on the tests, which provides the reliability coefficient of one-half the length of the test. The Spearman-Brown formula is used to determine the reliability of the full length test. It is usually represented as

$$r_{12} = \frac{2r_{\frac{1}{2}\,\frac{1}{2}}}{1 + r_{\frac{1}{2}\,\frac{1}{2}}}$$

r_{12} represents the estimated reliability of the whole test

r   represents the obtained correlation between the two half-tests

A coefficient of internal consistency based on the split-half method is a valid estimate of the reliability of a test if it is constructed according to appropriate principles of test construction. The split-half method should not be used with tests where speed is the prime factor.

2. *Kuder-Richardson Reliability Coefficient.* The Kuder-Richardson[27] method described here is a relatively simple procedure for obtaining an estimate of the reliability of a one-form test. The procedure is based on the assumption that the items are reasonably equal in difficulty and that the intercorrelations among the items approach high values.

When every item in a test has a high correlation with every other item in the test, it is said to have "interitem consistency"[28] or functional homogeneity. It becomes apparent that the procedure should not be used to determine the reliability of speed tests, and that, if the test does not possess functional homogeneity, the estimated reliability coefficient will be more conservative than if the split-half method were used.

The Kuder-Richardson formula (20) that is extensively used is:

$$r_{tt} = \left(\frac{n}{n-1}\right)\left(\frac{\sigma_{tt}^2 - \Sigma pq}{\sigma_t^2}\right)$$

r_{tt}:   estimated reliability

n: number of items in the test

σ_t: standard deviation of the test

σ_t^2:   variance of the test

p: proportion of persons passing each item

q: proportion of persons failing each item

Σ_{pq}:   sum of each of the products of pq for each item

Reliability coefficients should not be interpreted as absolute and fixed values that can be used as a "yardstick" in any situation. The interpretations of reliability coefficients correspond to the interpretation of coefficients of correlation.

27. Kuder, G. F. and M. W. Richardson: "The Theory of the Estimation of Test Reliability," *Psychometrika*, 2:151-160, September, 1937.

28. Freeman, F. S.: *Theory and Practice of Psychological Testing*, 3rd ed. New York, Holt, Rhinehart and Winston, 1962, p. 77.

Standard Error of Measurement

The reliability of a test may also be inferred from the standard error of a score, also called standard error of measurement (σ_{meas}). When the reliability of a test is relatively low, the standard error of measurement is larger. The concept of standard error of measurement takes into consideration both the standard deviation of the population for which the test reliability was established and the reliability coefficient established for the test.

Formula for Standard Error of Measurement

The formula used to calculate an estimate of the standard error of measurement is:

$$\sigma_{meas} = \sigma_{dist} \sqrt{1 - r_{tt}}$$

σ_{dist}: standard deviation of the distribution of scores for a given population

r_{tt}: reliability of the test

σ_{meas}: standard error of an individual score or the standard error of measurement

The size of the score units used to calculate the standard deviation of the distribution of scores influences the size of the standard error of measurement.[29] This factor must be observed when comparing the reliability of two or more tests. The reliability coefficient of two tests, X and Y, could be the same, but the standard error of measurement of Test X may be considerably larger than that of Test Y as the score units used to calculate the standard deviation for Text X may have been larger.

Application of Standard Error Measurement

Let us assume that the coefficient of reliability for Test W is .864 as obtained from a large group of individuals and the standard deviation of the scores for that group is 6.75. We wish to find the σ_{meas} or the standard error of an individual score. Substitutions of these values in the appropriate formula would be represented as follows:

$$\sigma_{meas} = \sigma_{dist} \sqrt{1 - .864}$$
$$= 6.75 \sqrt{.136}$$
$$= 6.75 \times .369$$
$$= 2.49$$

29. *Test Service Bulletin* 50, "How Accurate is a Test Score," New York, The Psychological Corporation, June, 1956.

An individual student obtained a score of 57 on Test W. We have no way of knowing his "true" score unless we could administer a large number (perhaps 100 or more) of different forms of the test. This theoretically would give us an extremely close estimate. However, we are able to interpret his score in terms of confidence bands. We can be almost certain that his "true" score would lie somewhere between three standard errors above and below his obtained score of 57. Consequently 3 $\times$ 2.49 or 7.47 may be added to and subtracted from 57 which gives us a range of 49.53 to 64.47. We may be highly confident that his "true" score lies somewhere between 49.53 and 64.47. We can be "reasonably confident" that his "true" score lies somewhere between 52.02 and 61.98 (2 $\times$ 2.49 = 4.98; 57 — 4.98 to 57 + 4.98). If we were to pursue the situation further, we could use the limits of one standard error above and below the student's score which would give us a confidence band of 54.51 to 59.49. Perhaps we could be "fairly confident" that the student's true score lies somewhere between the score values of 54.51 to 59.49.

FACTORS THAT AFFECT TEST RESULTS

There are a number of factors that should be considered when testing instruments are selected or that should be recognized when the tests are used. The characteristics of tests described previously are obviously important. There are other factors that must be recognized and observed or the measuring instruments with the best of characteristics may produce invalid and erroneous results, along with wasted efforts in conducting the evaluation program.

The scores obtained represent mostly the knowledge, ability, and information the examinees possess. There is always some error of measurement inherent in the measuring instrument.

Test results may be influenced by errors in administration, conversions and interpretations, poor quality pencils when machine scoring is used, physical conditions or environment during administration, and adequacy or appropriateness of norms.

GENERAL REFERENCES

Cronbach, Lee J.: *Essentials of Psychological Testing*, 2nd ed. New York, Harper and Brothers, 1960, pp. 96-109, 126-153.
Ebel, Robert L.: *Measuring Educational Achievement*, Englewood Cliffs, N. J., Prentice-Hall, 1965, pp. 388-392.

Greene, Harry A. *et al.*: *Measurement and Evaluation in the Elementary School.* New York, Longmans, Green and Co., 1953, pp. 385-389.

Johnson, Palmer O. and Robert W. B. Jackson: *Introduction to Statistical Methods.* New York, Prentice-Hall, 1953, pp. 308-316.

Noll, Victor H.: *Introduction to Educational Measurement.* Boston, Houghton Mifflin, 1957, pp. 66-84.

Remmers, H. H. and N. L. Gage: *Educational Measurement and Evaluation*, Rev. ed. New York, Harper and Brothers, 1955, pp. 131-144.

Standards for Educational and Psychological Tests and Manuals. Washington, D. C., American Psychological Association, Inc., 1966.

Test Service Bulletin, No. 44, The Psychological Corporation, May, 1952.

Test Service Bulletin, No. 50, The Psychological Corporation, June, 1956.

11 THE SCHOOL TESTING PROGRAM

W HAT does a school "testing program" represent? It should be an outline of intended action or an outline of the order of steps of events to be pursued within a more comprehensive total evaluation program. Evaluation is an integral part of instruction. Some form of evaluation is imperative whether it be in industry or in academic situations. In many instances it is subtle and indirect.

Since the 1920's many valuable tests have been constructed in the areas of general scholastic aptitude and academic achievement. In more recent years, particularly since World War II, special aptitude tests, personality, interest and other types of inventories and rating scales have been developed. At this point we will be concerned more specifically with the use of general scholastic aptitude and achievement tests as two basic components in a school testing program.

SCHOLASTIC APTITUDE AND ACHIEVEMENT TESTS

Teachers and guidance personnel are prone to consider scholastic aptitude and achievement tests as two distinctly different types of tests. This categorization may be somewhat misleading. Achievement tests are designed to measure knowledge, information and skills that may be learned within (in formal courses) or outside the classroom. Scholastic aptitude tests are designed to measure verbal reasoning and/or nonverbal reasoning. In the verbal reasoning test, words and numbers are used while in the nonverbal tests no words are used in the content of the test but the directions for administration may be either verbal or in pantomime. In the nonverbal test the emphasis is on the application of mental ability to new situations.

Except for transfer of identical elements, good scholastic aptitude tests are intended to be relatively unaffected by instruction.[30, 31]

30. *The Manchester Guardian Weekly*, Vol. 44, No. 14, April 3, 1952, p. 12.
31. *Effects of Coaching on Scholastic Aptitude Test Scores*, Educational Testing Service, Princeton, New Jersey, 1965.

Scholastic aptitude tests are used to make predictions of future academic achievement more accurate, while achievement tests are designed to evaluate what has been taught or learned. It should be recognized that achievement tests are an important means of predicting more or less immediate success in a given subject matter area.

Group tests of mental ability designed for the primary grades are essentially nonverbal tests. The difference between some nonverbal group tests and reading readiness tests is comparatively slight. The line of demarcation between the content of verbal scholastic aptitude tests and some achievement tests, particularly those in the area where reading is involved, become less distinct as development progresses through the upper grades and into the level of college admission tests. Examples of such tests are several subtests of the Iowa Tests of Educational Development, the Sequential Tests of Educational Progress, American College Testing Program, and a number of reading tests.

GROUP TESTING PROGRAM

There must be a need and a purpose for any kind of testing program. The questions "What tests make a good testing program?" or "What would make a good IQ test and achievement test battery to use?" have not become obsolete. One test is one too many if there is not a planned purpose for its use.

It is essential that there be a definite understanding as to why the tests are to be administered. The value of any testing program depends directly upon the use that is to be made of the results obtained. Use, interpretation, and application of test results to appraise and improve instruction and to help the individual to more adequately help himself are the basic elements in and functions of a real testing program in education. Industry is more directly concerned with selection, classification, and placement.

OBSERVATIONS PERTAINING TO A TESTING PROGRAM

The standardized testing program should follow a planned schedule to facilitate the charting of progress from kindergarten through grade twelve. Test batteries are also available that are designed to measure achievement and ability at the junior college level.

The content of scholastic aptitude tests is seldom questioned by those who use the tests in the elementary school grades or at the high school level. More attention is given to format, ease of scoring, conversion of scores, etc. However, in the case of achievement tests, one frequently hears the criticism that the test contains questions pertaining to content that was not taught. Standardized achievement tests are not designed to measure achievement based on one specific curriculum or course of study. The questions in a good achievement test pertain to concepts based on the theory of social utility. This means that the test items sample concepts or are based on areas of learning including knowledge, information, and basic skills that one could reasonably expect members of a society to know at a given age or grade level. If one wishes to observe how well the learner has mastered a relatively narrow course of study or a specific curriculum, an informal test should be constructed.

A good evaluation program makes it imperative that a standardized testing program be utilized. The standardized testing program should be of value to the teacher, curriculum director, administrator, and school counselor. Test scores help to make predictions more accurate but test scores should not be the sole basis upon which decisions are made. Test scores are an important consideration along with a variety of other quantitative and qualitative observations.

Local norms are established in many school systems. This makes possible a more comprehensive interpretation of test results. Norms established locally may be of one or more types. As pointed out in previous chapters it is possible to establish local norms in terms of grade placements, percentiles, stanines, or other standard scores.

PREDICTION OF FUTURE ACHIEVEMENT

As students progress through the various grade levels, including the elementary school grades, high school, and college, the problem of prediction becomes progressively more complicated as more variables occur or are "created" by and for the student. In very recent years more emphasis is again being placed on past achievement (grades) as a predictor of future performance.

Throughout approximately the first three grades the mental ability tests administered usually consist of nonverbal content. A good nonverbal test, if properly administered and interpreted, will give a good indication of the pupil's academic potential. However, as the pupils progress through the grades, learning difficulties of various kinds develop which may be directly or indirectly related to interest, attitude, personality, and motivation of behavior in general. The evidence seems to indicate that very few nonverbal mental ability tests are administered after the child enters the fourth grade. The gap between academic potential and achievement tends to widen. This is suggestive of the importance of testing and remedial work during the pre-high school and pre-college years that will help narrow the gap between academic potential and achievement or performance.

Comparatively recent past achievement is a good predictor of achievement for the immediate future. This, however, is not necessarily an indication of what the individual is capable of achieving. It may be that he is satisfied with his level of work and that he has not acquired the necessary knowledge and information to work at a higher level or a level that is commensurate with his capacity or academic potential. Consequently, other things being equal, we are reasonably confident that his performance in the near future will be approximately on the same level as it was in his immediate past.

TESTS AND WHEN TO TEST

Basically the function of a testing program is to improve instruction. The administration of standardized tests should be started early in the academic life of the child. The academic level at which various standardized tests are administered depends somewhat upon the type of plan under which the school system operates. It may be grades eight:four; six:six; six:three:three, or some other combination or modification of the educational structure.

Following is a schedule that is not necessarily ideal but it has been found reasonably adequate for the "average" school system.

1. Primary Grades (1-3)
    Reading Readiness Test: End of kindergarten or beginning of Grade 1
    Reading Achievement Test: End of Grade 1
    Mental Ability Test (academic potential): Beginning of Grade 2
    Achievement Test: Beginning of Grade 2
    Achievement Test: Beginning of Grade 3
    Sociometric Inventory: Before midyear of Grade 3
2. Intermediate Grades (4-6)
    Achievement Test: Beginning of Grade 4

Mental Ability Tests: Grade 4
Achievement Test: Beginning of Grade 5
Basic Study Skills: Grade 5
Personality Inventory (analytical nature rather than "diagnostic" or "clinical"): Grade 5
Verbal Mental Ability Test: Grade 6
*Nonverbal Mental Ability Test: Grade 6

3. Junior High School (7-9)
Achievement Test: Beginning of Grade 7
Achievement Test: Beginning of Grade 8
Verbal Mental Ability Test: Grade 8
Nonverbal Mental Ability Test: Grade 8
Interest Inventory (broad areas type): Grade 9

It is not essential that comprehensive batteries be administered at the various levels indicated above. In many instances a "partial battery" will serve the purpose very well. The partial battery usually consists of reading, arithmetic, language and spelling in one booklet.

A reading readiness test should be administered one or two weeks before the end of the kindergarten school year. If the reading readiness test is not administered at the end of the kindergarten year it should be administered in the first grade several days after the opening of the fall semester. The test need not be of a clinical nature nor should it be too brief. There are several good analytical reading readiness tests that provide useful information for the teacher. The test should not be so brief that it is of value only for coarse grouping, nor does it need to be so detailed that it could be used as a clinical instrument.

There is much variation in the testing that is done at the high school level. Some testing program directors or committees prefer to administer a complete battery of subject matter tests toward the end of grade nine and a more abbreviated battery (bound in one booklet or individual subject tests) in grade twelve. In some high schools only standardized tests designed for college admission purposes are used. The students who do not plan to attend college are given no tests. The school records should show test results for all students. Also, school officials should have available statistical data that show how

---

*A test that has been shown to be relatively free from verbal learning and general knowledge.

the school system test results compare with national or regional norms. These data can be obtained by means of periodic surveys of a systematic nature involving the entire school system. Such a survey may be made in lieu of some of the tests listed, particularly when a partial battery is used.

Comparatively little is done with interest and special aptitude tests beyond that of mechanical or perfunctory observations in the sum total evaluation programs. Apparently little consideration is given to technical courses or vocational education. A report of the National Advisory Council on Vocational Education[32] indicates that relatively small funds are allocated for vocational education programs. It is pointed out further that in the near future many more job opportunities will be available to the technically or vocationally trained persons.

It is becoming more and more obvious that interviews, surveys, aptitude tests, and interest questionnaires play an important part in the evaluation program beginning in some cases at the junior high school level. The available instruments should be considered in guiding the student's education in high school. If he plans to continue his formal education beyond high school the counseling should be started before he enrolls in a junior college or four year college. In counseling with college freshmen it becomes fairly evident that in many cases it was taken for granted that education in high school was directed toward the academic (liberal arts) curriculum.

There are numerous "career information" or "occupational briefs" that should be made available to the student to make it possible for him to better help himself. These sources of information should be used in conjunction with the data accumulated by means of the techniques listed above. This does not mean that decisions should be made for the students. The student should be provided with information that will help him to explore various possibilities and to select a field of education that will best prepare him for a career.

SUPPLEMENTARY TESTS AND EVALUATION INSTRUMENTS

There are several evaluation instruments that can be of help in acquiring information about and for the individual student. Applica-

32. *Education Recaps*, Vol. 9, No. 1, Educational Testing Service, Princeton, New Jersey, October, 1969.

tion of such instruments and procedures for observations can expedite the effectiveness with which learning may take place.

Some aids that can make an evaluation program more comprehensive and thus facilitate the learning process are:

1. *Handwriting Scales.* The scales for lower primary grades are usually in manuscript form. Very good cursive handwriting scales are available for intermediate and upper grades (e.g. Ayres Scale and others).

2. *Spelling Scales.* Valid spelling scales in the form of pre-tests and post-tests can be constructed by the classroom teacher. The New Iowa Spelling Scale[33] serves as a good example of how this can be done.

3. *Sociometric Studies.* Sociometric studies can be used to good advantage in the upper primary and intermediate grades. They are useful in detecting isolates and making observations regarding with whom pupils like to work or play (see forms in appendix). Sociometric studies can help the teacher to obtain better communication and interaction among all pupils in a class or organized groups.

4. *Interest Inventories.* Interest inventories or questionnaires when used in the intermediate or upper elementary grades provide information that can be useful in motivating the behavior of pupils and facilitate caring for individual differences in learning. During the high school years more formal interest questionnaires and vocational preference inventories are applicable. At the junior and senior high school level they usually are of a relatively broad nature but will serve as guidelines for further exploration and study of occupations and professions. Many inventories are based on questions to which the student responds while some inventories are presented in pictorial form.

5. *Personality Inventories.* The application and interpretation of personality inventories has its limitations. This may be said for almost any evaluation instrument. But the use of personality questionnaires and inventories may be more hazardous. The instruments may vary from simple impersonal questions to such involved instruments as the MMPI and projective techniques which require the training and experience of a clinical psychologist. In terms of structure it may be said that the procedures range from the use of highly structured to unstructured techniques. In most schools where personality tests are used they are of the question type that pertain to the students' attitudes, perceptions, feelings and conduct.

6. *Basic Study Skills.* The use of tests that pertain to study skills can be valuable instruments for analyzing or detecting areas where students

33. Greene, Harry A.: Bureau of Educational Research and Service, State University of Iowa, Iowa City, Iowa.

may need help. The tests are available for grades 3-12. The content in a good study skills test is categorized to help point out strengths and weaknesses of individuals, as well as certain weaknesses in the instructional program. The areas usually tested are map reading, use of reference material; understanding or reading maps, graphs, tables; using the dictionary and the index; organizing content materials and knowing various sources to locate information and reference material.

7. *Aptitude Tests for Occupations.* A limited number of aptitude tests designed for vocational counseling have been available for the junior high school level since 1959. Aptitude tests for the ninth grade and up have been available since World War II. The use and application of such instruments makes it imperative that the services of knowledgeable counselors be available to the students.

ADMINISTRATION OF THE TESTING PROGRAM

After the evaluation instruments are chosen the program must be implemented.

1. The chairman of the evaluation committee must be a competent and well qualified person.

2. Provisions should be made for an in-service training program for teachers and staff. All staff members should be informed regarding changes and progress.

3. Careful consideration should be given to the kind of test summaries that should be provided and for whom they should be planned. Schools within a district should not be compared only on a statistical basis. There are numerous variables that may affect the scores obtained by pupils in a given school.

4. Persons who have test results for their students must know how to use and interpret scores correctly and in a meaningful manner. If test results are made available to the teachers in the form of pupil profiles, graphical representation, or charting of standard scores it is highly important that the teacher be able to interpret the data and convey to parents that which it is intended to express.

5. Strengths and weaknesses of individual pupils and the class as a whole should be observed. Such strengths and weaknesses should be studied not only for an individual or grade but for the entire school system.

6. A certain amount of advance planning is essential regarding mechanics of test administration. This includes distribution and collecting of answer sheets (if separate) keeping in mind that some answer sheets contain two or more subtests. Care must be exercised in the distribution, collection, and storage of test booklets.

7. A time schedule for the administration of tests should be agreed upon. The schedule of tests should be distributed among all persons administering the tests, to persons directing group activities, the persons responsible for fire drills, etc., to avoid interruptions and unnecessary absences from test sessions.

8. To expedite the administration of tests it may be well to provide a proctor for every 30 or 35 pupils.

9. All persons administering the tests should be thoroughly familiar with the manual of directions.

10. It is important that timing of the tests be done accurately. Norms for tests are based on accurate timing.

11. When tests are to be machine scored it is essential that the directions provided for marking responses be adhered to without exception. The students must limit their writing and response marks to the spaces provided. There must be no stray marks or "dots" of any kind elsewhere on the answer sheet. Such stray marks lead only to inaccurate scoring or in some cases scores of zero. Each sheet should be carefully scanned by the examiner before the sheets are packaged in preparation for scoring. Only the pencils recommended should be used by the students, not to do so may lead to error.

The testing program outlined in this chapter is based on the philosophy that fall testing will make it possible to discover individual pupil as well as group strengths and weaknesses. This will help to make the guidance work more effective. Analytical or diagnostic tests may be administered any time during the year when there is a need for them. Locally constructed tests, with norms, can be a valuable supplement to the school evaluation program.

GENERAL REFERENCES

Durost, Walter N.: "What Constitutes a Minimal Testing Program for Elementary and Junior High School," *Test Service Notebook*, No. 1, rev., New York, World Book Company.

Glossary of Measurement Terms. California Test Bureau, Del Monte Research Park, Monterey, California.

Lennon, Roger T.: "Selection and Provision of Testing Materials," *Test Service Bulletin*, No. 99, New York, Harcourt, Brace and World, Inc.

Prescott, George A.: "Test Administration Guide," *Test Service Bulletin*, No. 102, New York, Harcourt, Brace and World, Inc.

Thorndike, Robert L. and Elizabeth Hagen: *Measurement and Evaluation in Psychology and Education*, 2nd ed. New York, John Wiley and Sons, 1961, pp. 444-481.

12 GRAPHICAL INTERPRETATIONS OF TEST RESULTS

THE derived or converted and sometimes raw scores obtained from tests are usually listed in class list form or they may be placed on pressure-sensitized labels. The labels are then placed in cumulative record folders. There are potentials in psychological and educational test results that oftentimes are not utilized. A basic evaluation program should facilitate improvement of instruction and it should be an aid to finding strengths and weaknesses within the individual pupils as well as the strengths and weaknesses in learning areas for the entire classroom, building, or the school district. The profile method of presenting test score data permits readily observable areas of strengths and weaknesses.

All the data used in Figures 6 through 16 in this chapter are based on the actual test results obtained in an eighth grade at the end of the first semester of the school year. Figures 6 through 8 represent pupil number 13 on the class list. Figures 9 through 14 represent the first 20 pupils on the class list and Figures 15 and 16 represent data obtained from the entire class of 33 pupils in the Washington School.

INDIVIDUAL PUPIL PROFILE
Grade Placement

Since Mike of the Washington School took the test battery at the end of January which is halfway through the school year, we drop a perpendicular from a point .5 of the distance from grade 8 to grade 9 through as many rows as we have tests in the battery administered. The data in Figure 6 show that Mike obtained a raw score of 39 in reading comprehension. The appropriate conversion table in the test manual shows that a raw score of 39 is the equivalent of a score obtained by a ninth grader at the end of the second month of the school year. We should not say that Mike is the equivalent of a ninth grader at the end of the second month of the school year. According to the grade placement he obtained we may say that he is well above average among eighth graders.

Mike's strengths and weaknesses in broad subject matter areas can be readily observed. In spelling, his grade placement compares favorably with the grade placement obtained by an average fifth grader at the end of the first month of the school year.

Percentile Ranks

The data in Figure 7 show Mike's grade scores converted to percentile ranks by means of the appropriate table in the test manual. The profile is constructed on the basis of percentile ranks. We observe that Mike obtained his best score in arithmetic, part 1, and he obtained his lowest score in spelling. We may say that the percentile rank in arithmetic obtained by Mike shows that 58 percent of the normative population did not obtain a score as high as he did at the end of the first semester of the eighth grade. We may also say that 6 percent of the normative population did not obtain a score as high as Mike's score in spelling or that 94 percent of the normative population obtained scores higher than that obtained by Mike.

Stanine Scores

Stanine scores are perhaps among the best converted scores to show pupil achievement. The data in Figure 8 show Mike's obtained scores converted to stanines. The conversions, like those made above, are made by means of tables in the test manual which accompanies the test used.

The use of stanine scores makes possible an effective means of interpreting scores and conveying areas of strengths and weaknesses to pupils and parents. Grade placements or grade equivalents still are the most commonly used norms even though they can be quite misleading as indicated in the topic "Grade Placements."

PROFILES SHOWING GRADE PLACEMENTS, PERCENTILES, AND STANINES
Class Profiles

Figures 9, 10, and 11 contain the data and profiles for the Washington School, grade 8. Only the first 20 pupils on the class list are used for the purpose of illustrating the grade profiles.

Frequency distributions are set up for the 20 pupils for each of the subtests. The median score obtained on each subtest is calculated. The median score is converted to grade placements, percentile ranks, and stanines. The construction of the profiles is done as it was done for Figures 6, 7, and 8. We now have a graphic representation of strengths and weaknesses in subject matter areas for one eighth grade classroom in the building.

School Building Profiles

If there are two or more classrooms for a given grade a frequency distribution may be made for all the scores obtained for each test for a given building. The median (or mean) is then calculated for all the scores obtained for each subtest. As indicated above, the "average" scores can then be converted to grade placements, percentile ranks, or stanines. Profiles can then be made for the school building as was done for one classroom and illustrated by means of Figures 9, 10, and 11.

School District Profiles

The profile technique may be an effective means for the director of curriculum or the school administrator to observe strengths and weaknesses in subject matter areas for the entire school system. The reliability and validity of the tests selected are an important factor in any conclusions that may be drawn from the data and profiles.

The procedures used in constructing profiles on a district wide basis are similar to those described above except that the averages obtained for a given grade level and subject matter area are based on a composite frequency distribution for each grade level and subject matter area for the entire district.

The person in charge of a testing program, the curriculum committee, or whoever is responsible for coordinating the activities of the evaluation program, must make certain decisions. Some of these decisions may be concerned with the format of the profiles or what type profile to use. For example, should it be based on percentile ranks, stanines, or grade placements.

CLASS LIST PROFILE BY SUBJECT TO SHOW INDIVIDUAL DIFFERENCES

Class list profiles show rather clearly the differences in achievement among the various students in a given subject matter area. A comparison between Figures 6 and 12 will show the difference in format of construction.

Figures 12, 13, and 14 show profiles based on the first 20 students in the eighth grade from which the data for this chapter were obtained. Profiles are shown only for the reading test of the battery administered. Similar profiles can be made for any subtest of a battery. As indicated previously, teachers may have a preference for a certain type converted score.

TEST RECORD AND PROFILE CHART

NAME: Mike Rogers   TEST: Standardized Achievement Test   GRADE: 8.5   Dates: Mo. 1 Da. 15 Yr. 1968

TEST NAME AND FORM (or Sub-Test)	Sc.	G.P.	Grade Placements											
			1	2	3	4	5	6	7	8	9	10	11	12
Reading Comprehension	39	9.2												
Arithmetic Part 1	26	9.2												
Arithmetic Part 2	19	8.2												
Arithmetic Part 3	13	7.4												
Spelling	14	5.1												
Language	90	7.3												

Figure 6. Individual pupil profile showing grade placements.

TEST RECORD AND PROFILE CHART

NAME: Mike Rogers   TEST: Standardized Achievement Test   GRADE: 8.5   Date: Mo. 1 Da. 15 Yr. 1968

Percentile Ranks

TEST NAME AND FORM (or Sub-Test)	Gr. Sc.	P.R.
Reading Comprehension	92	56
Arithmetic Part 1	92	58
Arithmetic Part 2	82	42
Arithmetic Part 3	74	28
Spelling	51	06
Language	73	32

Figure 7. Individual pupil profile showing percentile ranks.

TEST RECORD AND PROFILE CHART

NAME: Mike Rogers   TEST: Standardized Achievement Test   GRADE: 8.5   DATE: Mo. 1 Da. 15 Yr. 1968

Stanines

TEST NAME AND FORM (or Sub-Test)	Gr. Sc.	Sta-nine	1	2	3	4	5	6	7	8	9
Reading Comprehension	92	5									
Arithmetic Part 1	92	5									
Arithmetic Part 2	82	5									
Arithmetic Part 3	74	4									
Spelling	51	2									
Language	73	4									

Figure 8. Individual pupil profile showing stanine scores.

TEST RECORD AND PROFILE CHART

NAME: Washington School   TEST: Standardized Achievement Test   Grade: 8.5   Date: Mo. 1   Da. 15   Yr. 1968

TEST NAME AND FORM (or Sub-Test)	Sc.	G.P.	1	2	3	4	5	6	7	8	9	10	11	12
							Grade Placements							
Reading Comprehension	36	8.4												
Arithmetic Part 1	20	7.8												
Arithmetic Part 2	20	8.5												
Arithmetic Part 3	16	8.5												
Spelling	32	9.0												
Language	101	8.9												

Figure 9. School building profile showing grade placements.

TEST RECORD AND PROFILE CHART

NAME: Washington School   TEST: Standardized Achievement Test   GRADE: 8.5 DATE: Mo. 1 Da. 15 Yr. 1968

Percentile Ranks

TEST NAME AND FORM (or Sub-Test)	Gr. Sc.	P.R.	0	1	2	5	10	20	30	40	50	60	70	80	90	95	98	99	100
Reading Comprehension	36	48																	
Arithmetic Part 1	20	32																	
Arithmetic Part 2	20	48																	
Arithmetic Part 3	16	46																	
Spelling	32	54																	
Language	101	54																	

Figure 10. School building profile showing percentile ranks.

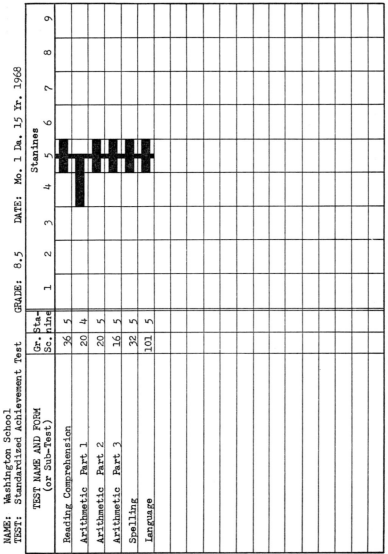

Figure 11. School building profile showing stanine scores.

TEST RECORD AND PROFILE CHART

NAME: Class List: Reading   TEST: Standardized Achievement Test   GRADE: 8.5   Date: Mo. 1 Da. 15 Yr. 1968

TEST NAME AND FORM (or Sub-Test)	Sc.	G.P.	1	2	3	4	5	6	7	8	9	10	11	12
Student #1	42	10.2												
Student #2	50	11.4												
Student #3	46	10.8												
Student #4	20	5.6												
Student #5	22	6.0												
Student #6	49	11.3												
Student #7	23	6.2												
Student #8	31	7.6												
Student #9	19	5.4												
Student #10	35	8.2												
Student #11	39	9.2												
Student #12	37	8.6												
Student #13	39	9.2												
Student #14	31	7.6												
Student #15	56	12.4												
Student #16	49	11.3												
Student #17	40	9.6												
Student #18	31	7.6												
Student #19	18	5.2												
Student #20	30	7.4												

Grade Placements

Figure 12. Class list profile showing grade placements.

TEST RECORD AND PROFILE CHART

NAME: Class List: Reading   TEST: Standardized Achievement Test   GRADE: 8.5   Date: Mo. 1 Da. 15 Yr. 1968

Percentile Ranks

TEST NAME AND FORM (or Sub-Test)	Gr. Sc.	P.R.
Student #1	102	64
Student #2	114	88
Student #3	108	77
Student #4	56	11
Student #5	60	14
Student #6	113	86
Student #7	62	16
Student #8	76	34
Student #9	54	10
Student #10	82	44
Student #11	92	56
Student #12	86	50
Student #13	92	56
Student #14	76	34
Student #15	124	98
Student #16	113	86
Student #17	96	58
Student #18	76	34
Student #19	52	08
Student #20	74	30

Figure 13. Class list profile showing percentile ranks.

TEST RECORD AND PROFILE CHART

NAME: Class List: Reading TEST: Standardized Achievement Test GRADE: 8.5 DATE: Mo. 1 Da. 15 Yr. 1968

TEST NAME AND FORM (or Sub-Test)	Gr. Sc.	Sta-nine
Student #1	102	6
Student #2	114	7
Student #3	108	7
Student #4	56	3
Student #5	60	3
Student #6	113	7
Student #7	62	3
Student #8	76	4
Student #9	54	2
Student #10	82	5
Student #11	92	5
Student #12	86	5
Student #13	92	5
Student #14	76	4
Student #15	124	9
Student #16	113	7
Student #17	96	5
Student #18	76	4
Student #19	52	2
Student #20	74	4

Stanines: 1 2 3 4 5 6 7 8 9

Figure 14. Class list profile showing stanine scores.

EXPECTANCY GRID

Stanine scores are quite functional when expectancy grids are constructed. Expectancy grids show rather clearly the relationship between academic potential and achievement of the student. The numbers used in constructing the graphic representation or scatter diagrams in Figures 15 and 16 represent the whole eighth grade class of the Washington School.

The data in Figure 15 are based on the stanine scores obtained by 33 students on a reading comprehension test and a verbal mental ability test of the omnibus type. The stanine values across the top of the grid represent the stanine scores obtained on the reading test. The stanine scores along the ordinate represent the stanine scores obtained on the verbal mental ability test. Student number 30 obtained a stanine score of 3 on reading and he obtained a stanine score of 6 on the verbal mental ability test. The scores on the whole tend to cluster along a lower left-upper right diagonal line. This seems to indicate that there is a fairly close relationship between the verbal mental ability test and the reading comprehension test (the Pearsonian r based on raw scores is .89, which is high and may raise a question regarding test construction).

Figure 16 contains data for the 33 students used in Figure 15. The reading comprehension test scores are those used in Figure 15 and the mental ability test scores were obtained from a nonverbal intelligence test with the scores shown in terms of stanines. The stanine scores are more scattered than in Figure 15 which indicates that the relationship between the two sets of scores is comparatively low (the Pearsonian r based on raw scores is .25). Students number 19, 24, and 30 are low in reading comprehension but they are quite high in the nonverbal intelligence test which may indicate that they have potential that is not being used and that they are having difficulties with reading comprehension. Student number 16 obtained stanine scores of 7 on verbal mental ability test and the reading comprehension test as shown in Figure 15. He scored comparatively low on the nonverbal test (Figure 16). One reason could be that he was not interested in the content of the nonverbal test. Such exceptions are to be expected.

Expectancy grids can be quite useful in identifying students who are not working up to their capacity. The problem of remedial work remains to be done.

PUPILS RANKED ON STANINE SCORE BASIS

SCHOOL____Washington_____ GRADE_____8_____

EXAMINER_____ DATE____January 15, 1968__

1. Test:___Reading Comprehension_____

2. Test:___Verbal Mental Ability_____

    Norms Used: 1. National (X)   Local ( )
                   2. National (X)   Local ( )

1.___Reading Comprehension_____

Stanine Scores

Verbal Mental Ability \ Stanine Scores	1	2	3	4	5	6	7	8	9
9								27	15
8					11		6		
7					10 12 31 25		2 3 21 16 28		
6			30	8 18	13 26 17 23 33	1			
5		19	29	14 20					
4		24	4 5 32 7	22					
3		9							
2									
1									

Figure 15. Expectancy grid for pupils in Washington School.

PUPILS RANKED ON STANINE SCORE BASIS

SCHOOL_____Washington_____GRADE_____8_____

EXAMINER_____DATE___January 15, 1968___

1. Test:____Reading Comprehension_____

2. Test:____Non-Verbal Intelligence Test_____

    Norms Used: 1. National (X)   Local ( )
                 2. National (X)   Local ( )

    1.___Reading Comprehension_____

Stanine Scores

2. Non-Verbal Intelligence Test / Stanine Scores	1	2	3	4	5	6	7	8	9
9					10			27	15
8		19	30	18	12 23		3 28		
7		24		8 20	11	1	2		
6			7 29 32	14 22	25 26 33 31		6 21		
5			4 5		13				
4		9			17		16		
3									
2									
1									

Figure 16. Expectancy grid for pupils in Washington School.

GENERAL REFERENCES

Durost, Walter N.: "The Characteristics, Use, and Computation of Stanines," *Test Service Notebook*, No. 23, New York, World Book Company.

Engelhart, Max D.: "Using Stanines in Interpreting Test Scores," *Test Service Notebook*, No. 28, New York, Harcourt, Brace and World, Inc.

Lyman, Howard B.: *Test Scores and What They Mean.* Englewood Cliffs, N. J., Prentice-Hall, pp. 138-150.

Stodola, Quentin: "How One School System Records and Interprets Test Scores: A Do-It-Yourself Kit for Teachers," *Test Service Notebook*, No. 89, New York, World Book Company.

Test Service Bulletin, No. 55, The Psychological Corporation, December, 1963.

APPENDICES

A CORRESPONDING VALUES OF STANDARD DEVIATIONS, VERBAL SCORES, STANINE SCORES, STEN SCORES, STANDARD SCORES, AND PERCENTILES OF NORMAL PROBABILITY CURVE

Standard Deviation	Verbal Score	Stanine Score	Sten Score	Standard Score	*Percentile
3.0				80	99.86
2.9				79	99.81
2.8				78	99.74
2.7				77	99.65
2.6				76	99.53
2.5				75	99.38
2.4				74	99.18
2.3			10	73	98.93
2.2	I			72	98.61
2.1		9		71	98.21
2.0			—	70	97.72
1.9				69	97.13
1.8				68	96.41
1.7		(1.75)	9	67	95.54
1.6				66	94.52
1.5	(1.5)	8	—	65	93.32
1.4				64	91.92
1.3				63	90.32
1.2		(1.25)	8	62	88.49
1.1				61	86.43
1.0	II	7		60	84.13
0.9				59	81.59
0.8				58	78.81
0.7		(0.75)	7	57	75.80
0.6				56	72.57
0.5	(0.5)	6	—	55	69.15
0.4				54	65.54
0.3				53	61.79
0.2		(0.25)	6	52	57.93
0.1				51	53.98
0.0	III	5	—	50	50.00
— 0.1				49	46.02
— 0.2				48	42.07
— 0.3		(— 0.25)	5	47	38.21
— 0.4				46	34.46
— 0.5	(— 0.5)	4	—	45	30.85
— 0.6				44	27.43

Standard Deviation	Verbal Score	Stanine Score	Sten Score	Standard Score	*Percentile
— 0.7				43	24.20
— 0.8		(—0.75)	4	42	21.19
— 0.9				41	18.41
— 1.0	IV	3	—	40	15.87
— 1.1				39	13.57
— 1.2				38	11.51
— 1.3		(— 1.25)	3	37	9.68
— 1.4				36	8.08
— 1.5	(— 1.5)	2	—	35	6.68
— 1.6				34	5.48
— 1.7				33	4.46
— 1.8		(— 1.75)	2	32	3.59
— 1.9				31	2.87
— 2.0			—	30	2.28
— 2.1				29	1.79
— 2.2		1		28	1.39
— 2.3	V			27	1.07
— 2.4			1	26	.82
— 2.5				25	.62
— 2.6				24	.47
— 2.7				23	.35
— 2.8				22	.26
— 2.9				21	.19
— 3.0				20	.135

*Adapted from E. D. Fitzpatrick: *Inferential Statistics Utility Tables.* Computer Services, Illinois State University, Normal, Illinois, by permission of the author.

B NORMAL DISTRIBUTION CHART

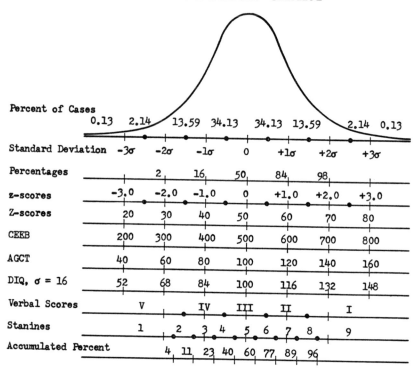

Percent of Cases	0.13	2.14	13.59	34.13		34.13	13.59	2.14	0.13
Standard Deviation	-3σ	-2σ	-1σ	0		+1σ	+2σ	+3σ	
Percentages		2	16	50		84	98		
z-scores	-3.0	-2.0	-1.0	0		+1.0	+2.0	+3.0	
Z-scores	20	30	40	50		60	70	80	
CEEB	200	300	400	500		600	700	800	
AGCT	40	60	80	100		120	140	160	
DIQ, σ = 16	52	68	84	100		116	132	148	
Verbal Scores	V		IV	III	II		I		
Stanines	1	2	3 4	5 6	7	8	9		
Accumulated Percent		4 11	23 40	60 77	89 96				

Mean and Standard Deviation of above Score Values

Score	Mean Set	Sigma Set
z-Score	0.0	1.0
Z-Score	50	10
CEEB	500	100
AGCT	100	20
DIQ, σ 16	100	16
Verbal Scores	III	1
Stanine	5	2

C WORK SHEET FOR ESTABLISHING PERCENTILE NORMS

1 Class Interval	2 Tabulations	3 f.	4 cf.	5 cf below i + .5f	6 *Percentile Rank

$$*\frac{\text{cf below i} + .5\ f}{N} \times 100$$

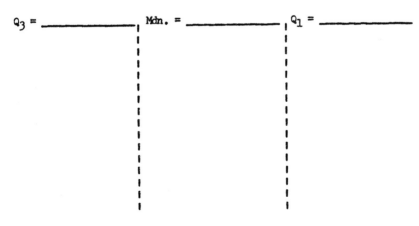

$Q_3 =$ _____, Mdn. = _____, $Q_1 =$ _____

123

D WORK SHEET FOR ESTABLISHING MEAN AND STANDARD DEVIATION

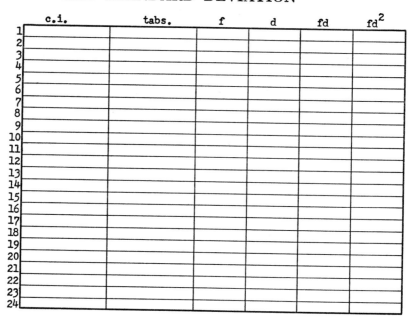

	c.i.	tabs.	f	d	fd	fd^2
1						
2						
3						
4						
5						
6						
7						
8						
9						
10						
11						
12						
13						
14						
15						
16						
17						
18						
19						
20						
21						
22						
23						
24						

$$M = AM + \frac{\Sigma fd}{N} i \qquad\qquad SD = i \sqrt{\frac{\Sigma fd^2}{N} - \left(\frac{\Sigma fd}{N}\right)^2}$$

$M = \underline{\hspace{1cm}} + \underline{\hspace{1cm}} \times \underline{\hspace{1cm}}$ $SD = \underline{\hspace{1cm}} \sqrt{\underline{\hspace{1cm}} - \left(\underline{\hspace{1cm}}\right)^2}$

$M = \underline{\hspace{1cm}} + \underline{\hspace{1cm}}$ $SD = \underline{\hspace{1cm}} \sqrt{\underline{\hspace{1cm}} - (\underline{\hspace{1cm}})^2}$

$M = \underline{\hspace{1cm}} + \underline{\hspace{1cm}}$ $SD = \underline{\hspace{1cm}} \sqrt{\underline{\hspace{1cm}} - (\underline{\hspace{1cm}})^2}$

$M = \underline{\hspace{1cm}} + \underline{\hspace{1cm}}$ $SD = \underline{\hspace{1cm}} \sqrt{\underline{\hspace{1cm}} - \underline{\hspace{1cm}}}$

$M = \underline{\hspace{1cm}}$ $SD = \underline{\hspace{1cm}} \sqrt{\underline{\hspace{1cm}} - \underline{\hspace{1cm}}}$

$SD = \underline{\hspace{1cm}} \sqrt{\underline{\hspace{1cm}}}$

$SD = \underline{\hspace{1cm}} \times \underline{\hspace{1cm}}$

$SD = \underline{\hspace{1cm}}$

E TABLE FOR CONVERTING YEARS AND MONTHS TO MONTHS

Yr-Mo	Mo	Yr-Mo.	Mo	Yr-Mo	Mo	Yr-Mo	Mo	Yr-Mo	Mo
5-0	60	8-10	106	12-8	152	16-6	198	20-4	244
5-1	61	8-11	107	12-9	153	16-7	199	20-5	245
5-2	62	9-0	108	12-10	154	16-8	200	20-6	246
5-3	63	9-1	109	12-11	155	16-9	201	20-7	247
5-4	64	9-2	110	13-0	156	16-10	202	20-8	248
5-5	65	9-3	111	13-1	157	16-11	203	20-9	249
5-6	66	9-4	112	13-2	158	17-0	204	20-10	250
5-7	67	9-5	113	13-3	159	17-1	205	20-11	251
5-8	68	9-6	114	13-4	160	17-2	206	21-0	252
5-9	69	9-7	115	13-5	161	17-3	207	21-1	253
5-10	70	9-8	116	13-6	162	17-4	208	21-2	254
5-11	71	9-9	117	13-7	163	17-5	209	21-3	255
6-0	72	9-10	118	13-8	164	17-6	210	21-4	256
6-1	73	9-11	119	13-9	165	17-7	211	21-5	257
6-2	74	10-0	120	13-10	166	17-8	212	21-6	258
6-3	75	10-1	121	13-11	167	17-9	213	21-7	259
6-4	76	10-2	122	14-0	168	17-10	214	21-8	260
6-5	77	10-3	123	14-1	169	17-11	215	21-9	261
6-6	78	10-4	124	14-2	170	18-0	216	21-10	262
6-7	79	10-5	125	14-3	171	18-1	217	21-11	263
6-8	80	10-6	126	14-4	172	18-2	218	22-0	264
6-9	81	10-7	127	14-5	173	18-3	219	22-1	265
6-10	82	10-8	128	14-6	174	18-4	220	22-2	266
6-11	83	10-9	129	14-7	175	18-5	221	22-3	267
7-0	84	10-10	130	14-8	176	18-6	222	22-4	268
7-1	85	10-11	131	14-9	177	18-7	223	22-5	269
7-2	86	11-0	132	14-10	178	18-8	224	22-6	270
7-3	87	11-1	133	14-11	179	18-9	225	22-7	271
7-4	88	11-2	134	15-0	180	18-10	226	22-8	272
7-5	89	11-3	135	15-1	181	18-11	227	22-9	273
7-6	90	11-4	136	15-2	182	19-0	228	22-10	274
7-7	91	11-5	137	15-3	183	19-1	229	22-11	275
7-8	92	11-6	138	15-4	184	19-2	230	23-0	276
7-9	93	11-7	139	15-5	185	19-3	231	23-1	277
7-10	94	11-8	140	15-6	186	19-4	232	23-2	278
7-11	95	11-9	141	15-7	187	19-5	233	23-3	279
8-0	96	11-10	142	15-8	188	19-6	234	23-4	280
8-1	97	11-11	143	15-9	189	19-7	235	23-5	281
8-2	98	12-0	144	15-10	190	19-8	236	23-6	282
8-3	99	12-1	145	15-11	191	19-9	237	23-7	283
8-4	100	12-2	146	16-0	192	19-10	238	23-8	284
8-5	101	12-3	147	16-1	193	19-11	239	23-9	285
8-6	102	12-4	148	16-2	194	20-0	240	23-10	286
8-7	103	12-5	149	16-3	195	20-1	241	23-11	287
8-8	104	12-6	150	16-4	196	20-2	242		
8-9	105	12-7	151	16-5	197	20-3	243		

F SOCIOMETRIC INFORMATION

School:_____ Grade:_____Month:_____Day:_____Year:____

DIRECTIONS: Place a "1", "2", and "3" in the right square to show the order of your choices of pupils with whom you would like to work or would like to have on a school committee with you.

Chooser \ Chosen	1.	2.	3.	4.	5.	6.	7.	8.	9.	10.	11.	12.	13.	14.	15.	16.	17.	18.	19.	20.	21.	22.	23.	24.	25.
1.																									
2.																									
3.																									
4.																									
5.																									
6.																									
7.																									
8.																									
9.																									
10.																									
11.																									
12.																									
13.																									
14.																									
15.																									
16.																									
17.																									
18.																									
19.																									
20.																									
21.																									
22.																									
23.																									
24.																									
25.																									
Total																									
One																									
Two																									
Three																									

G   SOCIOMETRIC INFORMATION

School:_____ Grade:_____ Month:_____ Day:_____ Year:_____

DIRECTIONS: Place a "1", "2", and "3" in the right square to show the order of your choices of pupils with whom you would like to play or have as your friends.

Chooser	Chosen 1. 2. 3. 4. 5.	6. 7. 8. 9. 10.	11. 12. 13. 14. 15.	16. 17. 18. 19. 20.	21. 22. 23. 24. 25.
1.					
2.					
3.					
4.					
5.					
6.					
7.					
8.					
9.					
10.					
11.					
12.					
13.					
14.					
15.					
16.					
17.					
18.					
19.					
20					
21.					
22.					
23.					
24.					
25.					
Total One Two Three					

H PUBLISHERS AND DISTRIBUTORS OF TESTS

1. American Guidance Service, Inc., Publisher's Building, Circle Pines, Minnesota 55014.
2. *Bobbs-Merrill Company, Inc. (The), 4300 East 62nd Street, Indianapolis, Indiana 46206.
3. *Bureau of Educational Research and Service, University of Iowa, Iowa City, Iowa 52240.
4. *Bureau of Publications, Teachers College, Columbia University, New York, New York 10027.
5. *California Test Bureau, Del Monte Research Park, Monterey, California 93940.
6. Center for Psychological Services, George Washington University, 1935 Eye Street, N.W., Washington, D.C. 20006.
7. Committee on Diagnostic Reading Tests, Inc., Mountain Home, North Carolina 28758.
8. Consulting Psychologist's Press, 577 College Avenue, Palo Alto, California 94306.
9. Educational Records Bureau, 21 Audubon Avenue, New York, New York 10032.
10. *Educational Testing Service, Rosedale Road, Princeton, New Jersey 08540.
11. Grune and Stratton, Inc., 381 Park Avenue, South, New York, New York 10016.
12. *Harcourt, Brace and World, Inc., 757 Third Avenue, New York, New York 10017 or 7555 Caldwell Avenue, Chicago, Illinois 60648.
13. Harlow Publishing Company, 212 East Gray Street, Norman, Oklahoma 73069.
14. *Houghton Mifflin Company, 1900 South Batavia Avenue, Geneva, Illinois 60143 or 53 West 43rd Street, New York, New York 10036.
15. *Institute for Personality and Ability Testing, 1602 Coronado Drive, Champaign, Illinois 61822.
16. Layton, Wilbur L., 3604 Ross Road, Ames, Iowa 50010 (OSU Intelligence Test).
17. Lyons and Carnahan, 407 East 25th Street, Chicago, Illinois 60616.
18. McKnight and McKnight, IAA Drive, Bloomington, Illinois 61701.
19. Mills Music, Inc., 1619 Broadway, New York, New York 10017.

*The sources marked with an asterisk publish or distribute a comparatively large number and variety of standardized tests.

20. Northwestern University Psycho-Educational Clinic, Evanston, Illinois 60201.
21. Personnel Press, Inc., 661 Maple Avenue, Greenwich, Connecticut 06830.
22. *Psychological Corporation (The), 304 East 45th Street, New York, New York 10017.
23. Psychometric Affiliates, 1743 Monterey, Chicago, Illinois 60643.
24. Research Foundation, 2801 West Bancroft Street, University of Toledo, Toledo, Ohio 63406.
25. *Science Research Associates, 259 East Erie Street, Chicago, Illinois 60611.
26. Slossen Educational Publications, 140 Pine Street, East Aurora, New York 14052.
27. Van Wagenen Psycho-Educational Research Laboratories, University of Minnesota, Minneapolis, Minnesota 55455.
28. *Western Psychological Services, 12031 Wilshire Blvd., Los Angeles, California 90025.
29. See also: Thorndike and Hagen: *Measurement and Evaluation in Psychology and Education*, 2nd ed. John Wiley and Sons, Inc., pp. 571-595, 605 Third Avenue, New York, New York 10016.

INDEX